opening ..

Penguin
LIVES

Simone Weil

A LIPPER™/ VIKING BOOK

FRANCINE DU PLESSIX GRAY

Simone Weil

A Penguin Life

A LIPPER™/ VIKING BOOK

VIKING

Published by the Penguin Group
Penguin Putnam Inc., 375 Hudson Street,
New York, New York 10014, U.S.A.
Penguin Books Ltd, 27 Wrights Lane, London W8 5TZ, England
Penguin Books Australia Ltd, Ringwood, Victoria, Australia
Penguin Books Canada Ltd, 10 Alcorn Avenue,
Toronto, Ontario, Canada M4V 3B2
Penguin Books (N.Z.) Ltd, 182–190 Wairau Road,
Auckland 10, New Zealand

Penguin Books Ltd, Registered Offices:
Harmondsworth, Middlesex, England

First published in 2001 by Viking Penguin,
a member of Penguin Putnam Inc.

1   3   5   7   9   10   8   6   4   2

Grateful acknowledgment is made for permission to reprint excerpts from the following
copyrighted works:

Simone Weil: An Intellectual Biography by Gabriella Fiori, translated by Joseph R.
Berrigan. Translation copyright © 1989 by The University of Georgia Press. Reprinted
by permission of The University of Georgia Press.

Simone Weil: A Life by Simone Pétrement, translated by Raymond Rosenthal.
Reprinted by permission of Librairie Arthème Fayard, Paris.

La Condition Ouvrière by Simone Weil. © Éditions Gallimard. Used by permission of
Éditions Gallimard, Paris.

Photographs courtesy of Sylvie Weil and Nicolette Schwartzman.

CIP data available

ISBN 0-670-89998-4

This book is printed on acid-free paper. ∞

Printed in the United States of America
Set in Bodoni Book
Designed by Francesca Belanger

To the memory of Lieutenant Bertrand du Plessix,

Forces Aériennes Françaises Libres,

1902–40

Heureux ceux qui sont morts, car ils sont retournés
Dans la première argile et la première terre.
Heureux ceux qui sont morts dans une juste guerre
Heureux les épis mûrs et les blés moissonnés. . . .
Heureux ceux qui sont morts dans une guerre antique
Heureux les vases purs et les rois couronnés.

Blessed are the dead, for they have returned
To original clay and primeval earth.
Blessed are those who died in a just war
Blessed the ripened sheaves and the harvested wheat. . . .
Blessed are those who died in an ancient war
Blessed are pure vessels and anointed kings.

—Charles Péguy

Contents

PART I: HOME

Simone Weil in Baden-Baden at age twelve

1. The Factory of Genius

_____

GROWING UP in Paris in the first decades of the twentieth century were two contented children from whose household all toys and dolls had been categorically banned. It had been their mother's intent to nurture their intellectual skills, and the gambit had obviously worked. The older child, André Weil, born in 1906, was solving the most advanced mathematical problems by the time he was nine; by the age of twelve he had taught himself classical Greek and Sanskrit and become an accomplished violinist. His sister, Simone, three years his junior, a strikingly beautiful girl with dark, limpid eyes, was reading the evening paper aloud to her family when she was five, and would master Greek and several modern languages in her early teens. The siblings often communicated with each other in spontaneously rhymed couplets, or in ancient Greek. When reciting scenes from Corneille or Racine they corrected each other with a slap in the face when one of them made a mistake or missed a beat. Theirs was a hermetic, rarified world—the young Weils' conversations, though never meant to exclude anyone, were so laced with literary and philosophical allusions that they were barely accessible to outsiders. Who could have guessed, for instance, that Simone's recitation of the lament for Hippolyte from Racine's *Phèdre* was meant to inform her

3

brother that she had completed her Latin composition and was ready to study Aeschylus with him as soon as he was finished with his differential calculus?

The Weils' saga begins, as so many do, with the myth of the perfectly happy family. The uncommon brilliance and talents of their son and daughter may have been the crowning glory of the Weils' cosseted lives, but it was hardly the only one. Dr. Bernard Weil's practice as an internist had thrived ever since he had opened it. His wife, Selma, was a dynamic woman who radiated intelligence and joie de vivre, and their mutual devotion was legendary. As for the early flowering of the Weil children's genius (how could one have wished for more amazing children?), Mme Weil was almost totally responsible. Dr. Weil—kind, loving, and thoroughly enlightened, but taciturn and easily overwhelmed by his forceful spouse—was far too busy with his medical practice, and let his wife make the major decisions concerning their children's education. Selma, also known in the family as "Mime," had much desired, in her youth, to become a doctor. Her father having forbidden her, for the usual patriarchal reasons, to go to medical school, she seemed to have rechanneled her vast energies and ambitions into her children's success. Because few educators were skilled enough, in her judgment, to stand up to her son's and daughter's formidable gifts, within a span of five years Simone and André would attend more than a half-dozen schools and be instructed by scores of private tutors. One might well say that the dominating Selma Weil was a genius factory of sorts, masterminding every move in her children's intellectual training, tapping every available educational resource to assure the fulfillment of their talents.

Mme Weil was as scrupulous about her children's physical well-being as she was about their education. A phobic dread of microbes ruled her household. The Weils were close friends of the eminent Russian-born microbiologist Élie Metchnikoff, a director of the Pasteur Institute, who had won the Nobel Prize in 1908 for his pioneering research on infectious diseases. Having picked up from the scientist, as André Weil later wrote, "a dread of germs which [Simone] would carry to an extreme,"[1] Mme Weil ruled that her children should not be kissed by anyone outside the immediate family. When she took her son and daughter onto a Paris bus she had them sit on the top deck so as to minimize any chance of infection. Compulsive hand-washing was another habit she imposed on her children. At mealtimes, if André and Simone needed to open a door after having washed their hands, they had to shove it open with an elbow. These phobias about food and germs would strongly affect Simone's psychic makeup. The word *dégoutant*, "disgusting," seems to have been frequently used by the Weils, and from the time she could talk she often said, "I am disgusting." By the time she was four she disliked being kissed, even by her parents, and for the rest of her life she displayed repulsion for most forms of physical contact. When she was five, a friend of her parents, a doctor, was so touched by her beauty that he leaned down to kiss her hand. Simone burst into tears and cried, "Water, water! I want to wash!!"[2]

Simone Adolphine Weil was born on February 3, 1909, in her parents' apartment on the Rue de Strasbourg, just south of the Gare de l'Est (since destroyed, the street was rebuilt as the Rue de Metz). When she was five her family moved to a larger flat on the Boulevard Saint-Michel. Her mother, née Salomea Reinherz (she had shortened her first name to

"Selma"), came from a wealthy family of Jewish business-men who had prospered in the import-export trade in many countries. Selma spent her first few years in Russia, which her parents left in the wake of the 1880s pogroms to move to Belgium. Hers was the more artistic side of the family. Her father wrote poetry in Hebrew, and her mother, who would live with the Weils until her death, was a gifted pianist. As for Dr. Bernard Weil, who was addressed by his children as "Biri," he came from a family of Jewish merchants that had been settled for generations in Strasbourg. His politics were mildly left of center, and he was an extreme secularist. He disliked talking about his Jewishness. This reluctance must have had its share of complexities, for his mother, who lived on in Paris into the 1930s, remained very pious. She kept a kosher kitchen and proclaimed that she would rather see her granddaughter die than marry a Gentile. When visiting her son's family, she would follow her daughter-in-law, Selma, into the kitchen and scold her for cooking foods that were contrary to Jewish dietary laws.

In this ritualistically hygienic family, Simone, who had been born a month premature, spent a very sickly infancy and childhood. When the baby was six months old, her mother continued to breast-feed her while recovering from an emergency appendectomy. Simone began to lose a great deal of weight and grew very ill. When she was eleven months old Mme Weil was persuaded to wean her, but Si-mone, in an early struggle of conflicting wills, refused to eat from a spoon. She became so thin that several doctors gave her up for lost; until the age of two she did not grow in height or weight, and had to be fed mush from bottles into which in-creasingly large holes were pierced. Reflecting, as an adult, on these early crises (which might have played a role in the severe eating problems she developed in adolescence), Simone sometimes speculated that she had been "poisoned" in infancy by her mother's milk: *"C'est pourquoi je suis tellement ratée,"* she'd say, "That's why I'm such a failure."[3]

Simone continued to be delicate throughout her childhood. At the age of three she took months to recover from her own appendectomy, which so traumatized her that for many years the sight of the Eiffel Tower, which she and her mother had had to pass on the way to the hospital, made her cry. Whenever a stranger came to visit her family, she even left the room in fear that he was a doctor. Her mother grew all the more obsessive about her daughter's health, pampering and cosseting the hypersensitive, moody child. "She is indomitable, impossible to control, with an undescribable stubbornness that neither her father nor I can make a dent in," she wrote a friend when her "Simonette" was five. "I certainly have spoiled her too much. . . . I can't help but fondle and kiss her much more than I should."[4]

Although they never rebelled overtly against their coddling parents, the young Weils clearly became very gifted at manipulating them. As they grew older they occasionally derided their exceptionally protected childhoods. One of their favorite pranks was to get on the bus without their socks on a cold winter day and go through their "neglected children" routine. Teeth chattering, shaking with mock shivers, they announced to concerned passengers that their neglectful parents did not even buy them any socks. ("You wretch!" a woman once shouted accusingly at Mme Weil.) Another good game was to go knocking at strangers' doors to beg for food, pleading that their parents were letting them "die of hunger" (they especially asked for sweets, which were forbidden in the Weils' home). On hearing of such jests

Dr. and Mme Weil were overcome with shame and indignation, and their offspring continued to act out their psychodramas all the more gleefully.

The advent of World War I, which put to rest the complacent myth of progress that had prevailed for over a century among Europe's liberal bourgeoisie, was the first pall cast on the young Weils' life. It was the critical event that thrust Simone out of the smug cocoon of her affluent childhood and gave her an inkling of what would become a central theme of her work—suffering or "affliction." The principal impact of the war on her own family was constant relocation. Mme Weil and her children followed Dr. Weil, who had been drafted into the army medical corps, to the towns of Neufchâtel, Mayenne, Laval, Chartres, renting spacious houses in each community to be close to his army quarters. It was during these war years that Simone's precocious political consciousness and her bent for self-sacrifice first became pronounced (at the age of three she had already turned down a wealthy relative's gift of a jeweled ring on the grounds that she "disliked luxury.") In 1916, when she was six years old, she decided that she wished to go without sugar because "the poor soldiers at the front" did not have any. That same year she adopted a "godson" at the front, a French custom during World War I, whereby families signed up to send food and clothing to underprivileged soldiers. By gathering and selling bundles of wood, Simone earned her own money to buy provisions for "her soldier." He came in 1917 to spend a leave with the Weils. Simone grew immensely fond of him. He died in action the following year, and she grieved greatly over this loss.

By the age of ten the intense little girl with the mass of

tangled black hair, who already read several newspapers a day, began to display her sensitivity to issues of justice and her sense of history. In 1919, at the Great War's end, she was appalled by the manner in which the Treaty of Versailles "humiliated the defeated enemy." A few years later she would write to a friend, "I suffer more from the humiliations inflicted by my country than from those inflicted upon her," noting that the Versailles Treaty cured her once and for all of any "naïve patriotism." A superdiligent student who displayed a particular fascination with world events, she seems to have followed the course of the Russian Revolution fairly closely and talked about it in school, for, upon being accused by a classmate that year of being a Communist, she defiantly replied: "Not at all; I am a Bolshevik." Issues of domestic justice were equally urgent. During a summer vacation, Simone, increasingly uncomfortable with the sense that she belonged to a very privileged elite, assembled the bellhops, chambermaids, desk clerks, and porters at the hotel where her family was staying, chided them that they worked too hard, and urged them to form a trade union.

A few months after the war's end, as her family was settling back into their apartment on Boulevard Saint-Michel, Mme Weil noticed that Simone was nowhere to be seen. She rushed downstairs with her housekeeper to see what Simone was up to. The ten-year-old was found in the thick of the labor union demonstrations being staged a few blocks down the avenue, marching alongside the workers as they sang the *Internationale* and shouted their demands for better wages and hours.

The year 1919, when her political consciousness began to flower, offered Simone yet other epiphanies. According to André Weil, it was then that the Weil children first learned that they were Jewish, a discovery that needs some elaboration. Both Dr. Weil, a professed atheist, and his wife exemplified the pattern of extreme assimilation that distinguished the progressive Jewish intelligentsia in France. This integration had to do, in part, with the Revolution of 1789, through which France became the first country in Europe to grant Jews rights of full citizenship, and which enabled them, in the following centuries, to rise to higher positions of eminence in the academic and political sphere than in any other European nation (philosopher Henri Bergson, sociologist Emile Durkheim, composer Jacques Halévy, Socialist premiers Léon Blum and Pierre Mendès-France, among them). Notwithstanding the acutely anti-Semitic currents later made manifest by the Dreyfus affair and the right-wing group Action Française, France's early pattern of tolerance inspired its Jewish community to display its patriotic fidelity by blending totally into the national melting pot. "No Jew prays harder for his country than a French Jew . . . ,"[5] in the words of the contemporary French Jewish scholar Alexandre Alder. "This nation is the emancipator of Jews, and will provoke among them torrents of eternal devotion."[6]

The intensity of Simone Weil's patriotism—a critical but savagely committed patriotism that may have shaped her destiny more deeply than that of any twentieth-century writer—might be seen in the light of this uniquely French pattern of assimilation. The same need for assimilation led Dr. and Mme Weil to decide that their children should not be told the difference between Jews and Gentiles until they had reached a fairly mature age. Mme Weil had suffered considerably from anti-Semitism during her youth in Central Europe and often stated her "profound desire to integrate herself into French society."[7] As an Alsatian Jew, Dr.

Weil had had to deal with a double level of alienation: Neither Jews nor Alsatians were ever seen as genuine "Français de France." Simone's extremely tortured emotions about Judaism and her acute sense of deracination—her fundamental inability to experience a sense of "belonging" to any organization or milieu—are more understandable when seen in the light of these very complex family attitudes.

There was yet another way in which the year 1919–20 was an emotional turning point for Simone: It was the time when she had to confront, and accept, the genius of her brother, André, who was to become one of the two or three most prominent mathematicians of the postwar era.

As is the case with most mathematicians, André's gifts had flowered very early. He had come to his vocation at the age of eight, when he found a geometry book at an aunt's house and studied it as an entertainment. Seeing him working for days on end on mathematical problems, his parents took away papers and pencils so that he could get back to occupations more "normal" to his age; but they dropped this taboo when they noticed that he continued to write out equations on cement sidewalks. At the age of twelve he was solving mathematical problems beyond the doctoral level and was reading Plato and *The Iliad* in the original Greek. At the age of fourteen, three years below the minimum age required by the government, he obtained a special dispensation to take his *bachot*—the state-sponsored baccalaureate exam—and passed it with the highest scores in the nation. He then started preparing for the examinations that would allow him entrance to the École Normale Supérieure, the prestigious graduate school that has trained much of France's intellectual elite—Henri Bergson, Jean-Paul Sartre, Claude

Lévi-Strauss, and Georges Pompidou, among scores of others. Such preparations are traditionally made through a few years of cramming school called *cagne* (ironic student argot for "laziness," also spelled "khāgne")—intermediate institutions attached to the best lycées—but André whizzed through *cagne* in one year instead of the usual two, passing the exams that allowed him access to the scientific division of Normale with, again, the highest scores in France.

How would Simone—immensely competitive and ambitious by nature, always striving to attain first rank among her peers—accommodate herself to the fact of her brother's all-too-evident genius? Any sense of rivalry the siblings felt toward each other was bound to be made all the more complex by their great mutual devotion. Notwithstanding her distaste for physical contact, Simone was extremely receptive to other expressions of tenderness, and adulated her brother all the more because of the affection he lavished upon her. From their early childhood on, André had done all he could to bring his brilliant but slightly less precocious sister into his own rarefied sphere. At the age of eight, for instance, he had decided that as a birthday present to his father he would teach his five-year-old sister to read. He made her work for long stretches, sometimes six hours in a row—even their walks were devoted to practicing spelling—and accomplished his goal in a matter of weeks. "Simone . . . follows André everywhere," their mother reported during a summer vacation when her daughter was five. "She's interested in his every move . . . he protects her, he helps her clamber out of tight spots, he often gives way to her."[8] As they were growing up, André continued to share with Simone what he was learning in school and on his own, introducing her to Plato, explaining astronomy to her on the tram. The siblings communicated on such a level of intellectual virtuosity that on one occasion, a woman sitting behind them on the bus got off, angrily exclaiming, "How can anyone train children to be such parroting savants!"

Relations between the siblings were not perpetually harmonious, however. The scholarly silence of their quarters gave way on occasion to a muffled, thumping sound. Mme Weil came rushing into their rooms, and found Simone and André locked in physical battle: "They fought in the deepest silence, so as not to attract our attention . . ." Mme Weil recalled. "We heard only a shuffling; never a shout. When we came into the room, they'd be pale and shaking, each holding the other by the hair."[9] But such squabbles—one particular spat began when Simone refused to lend her brother her copy of Racine because it contained passages about sex she felt he shouldn't see—were infrequent. Most times the Weil children maintained the tone of affectionate serenity and elevated intellectual pursuit established by their parents. Voices were seldom raised, divisive or sensitive issues (such as Jewishness) were avoided. Though "Biri" is rarely heard about in family accounts—he is not so much absent from family affairs as eclipsed by his wife's dominating presence—the Weils' mutual devotion continued to be exemplary. One of their idiosyncracies, at mealtimes, was to save the morsel of meat or fowl they each knew the other most fancied—he saved her the tidbit of lamb nearest the bone, she saved him morsels of the chicken's second joint—with the result, their children teased, that each of them might end up with the food they liked least. (Mme Weil, a hefty woman, was a gourmet who put a great importance on cuisine and fussed a lot about the freshness and healthiness of different foods; this, too, might have been a factor in the eating disorders Simone was to develop in her teens.)

Other preferred topics of conversation at the Weils' dinner table—music, literature, and André's favorite hobby, the collecting of rare editions of Greek and Latin texts—were occasionally held in the family's second languages, German and English. It was a highly cosmopolitan family. Mme Weil, who had inherited a tidy income from her prosperous merchant father, loved to travel, and several times a year devised ingenious vacations for the family to enjoy together. In fact, one is bound to be struck by the variety of fashionable, luxurious vacations the commanding Mme Weil planned for her family. Spending substantial sums on their travel, the Weils took off, not only on summer vacations but on any other major holidays—Christmas, Easter, Pentecost, All Souls' Day—to a variety of glamorous destinations, such as biking trips in the Tyrol or hiking treks in the Black Forest. It might have indeed been difficult for Simone and André to take that essential step of a healthy adolescence—a measured rebellion against parental authority—with a father and mother as eminently generous, progressive, loving, and enlightened as Dr. and Mme Weil. They even knew how to use that potent tool of emotional release, humor, to keep their kids in line; for along with a merciless outpouring of intellect there was a lot of affectionate teasing, at the Weils' dinner table, about everyone's foibles. André had not studied long enough hours today to be content, so the ribbing might go. Papa had not sufficiently exhausted himself working at his office to be happy tonight. Maman had not organized the lives of others as much as she would have liked. Simone had not suffered enough to feel worthy. This last allusion was bound to be brought up frequently, for it was clear, by the time she was fourteen, that the most singular trait of Simone's character was her almost pathological receptiveness to the sufferings of others, and her strong tendency to cultivate her own.

Simone had had a share of heartaches to deal with as she was growing up in the postwar years. They were in part precipitated by the obstacles she confronted during her first years of formal schooling. She had just turned ten in January 1919, when her father was demobilized and the family finally returned to a stabler life in Paris. Her gifts were less focused and less evident than her brother's, and consequently her studies had suffered more than his during the Weils' nomadic war years. Her problems may have also been aggravated by her mother's overzealous response to them: The overbearing finickiness with which Mme Weil supervised her daughter's education was displayed in the following years. She had Simone finish that year with private tutors, and in the fall enrolled her at a prominent girls' school, the Lycée Fénelon, where—two years younger than her average classmate—she was placed into the grade in which Latin and Greek were begun. "Physically, she was a little child, unable to use her hands, but of extraordinary intelligence," a former schoolmate recalls. "She looked as if she belonged to another order of being, and her mind didn't seem to belong to our age or our milieu. She felt like a very old soul."[10]

Although this "old soul" put enormous energy into her work and excelled at it (she outshone her classmates in everything but cartography and drawing, in which she scored a resounding zero), she easily grew tired from the effort because of a specific handicap: Her hands, disproportionately small for her fairly large-boned body, were unusually weak and maladroit. So she wrote sloppily and slowly, never finishing in time with her classmates. Because of her clumsiness, Simone, aged ten, began the habit of waking up in the middle of the night to finish her homework. This was the first of many health-weakening obligations she would impose on herself throughout her life, and out of sheer exhaustion she often had to spend days at a time in bed. She grew so tired, in fact, that the following school year, 1920–21, Mme Weil decided to take Simone out of the school system altogether and have her tutored at home again. She returned to Fénelon in the autumn of 1921, when she was twelve, but remained there for only three months of the first semester, because Mme Weil judged her homeroom teacher to be too "critical and ironic" in her attitude. Simone finished the winter term with tutors, and in the spring semester was switched to another distinguished girls' school. But there a new obstacle arose: Mme Weil feared that Simone, who was inevitably first in her class, was paid "too many compliments" by her teachers. So she again dropped out for the rest of the semester, concentrating on studying classical Greek at home. Mme Weil worried about Simone's unease with formal schooling and continued to contrast her problems with her brother's easy successes. André was always calm, she commented; exams and assignments were a true joy to him because "without being the least vain . . . he is sure of himself. . . . Simone, on the other hand, is always inclined to mistrust herself."[11]

Simone, now aged thirteen, returned to the Lycée Fénelon in October 1922, having decided to stick it out with the "critical and ironic" teacher who had incited her to drop out the previous year. This time the same teacher complained that Simone, who was far more advanced than her classmates, agitated her comrades by demanding that the entire class be assigned to learn Racine's *Athalie* by heart! It was that very autumn, as she endured her difficulties at Fénelon, that Simone began to suffer from the acute migraines that would plague her for most of her life. And it was later in that same school year that she experienced her first severe emotional crisis. By this time André had been accepted at the École Normale Supérieure. Simone's first acute depression seems to have had a great deal to do with her growing awareness of her brother's superiority and her parents' pride in his precocious achievements. Here is how she described the crisis, which was signaled by those feelings of extreme worthlessness common to most young anorexics, in a 1941 letter to a friend:

> At fourteen I fell into one of those fits of bottomless despair that come with adolescence, and I seriously thought of dying because of the mediocrity of my natural faculties. The extraordinary gifts of my brother, who had a childhood and a youth comparable to Pascal's, brought my own inferiority home to me.[12]

The comparison of her brother to the mathematical prodigy, physicist, and religious thinker Blaise Pascal (1623–62) is highly significant. Like André, the multifaceted Pascal was a virtuoso who had mastered the highest principles of mathematics by the time he was fourteen; and he was exceptionally close to his brilliant younger sister, who was a literary prodigy. Like Simone, both of the Pascal siblings would have major religious conversions in their early adulthood, and Jacqueline Pascal went on to be a nun at Port-Royal, the center of the ascetic Catholic reform movement known as Jansenism. Since Pascal early became one of Simone's favorite writers—she already knew scores of his *Pensées* by heart by the time she was fourteen, and later would write that she had "virtually learned to read through reading Racine and Pascal"—one is led to wonder whether there might have been a trace of Pascalian mimesis in Simone's self-image: "I did not mind having no visible successes," she continued in her letter of 1941. "What did grieve me was the idea of being excluded from that transcendent realm to which only the truly great minds have access, and wherein truth abides. I preferred to die rather than live without that truth."

She began to see some hope in reaching that "truth" through an attitude of extreme perseverance and "concentrated attention" toward her schoolwork. She passed her first *bachot* with high grades; and to prepare for her far more difficult second *bachot*, her mother sent her to yet another lycée whose star professor, a noted authority on Plato and on German idealism, immediately recognized Simone's gifts and lavished particular attention on her. It was under his tutelage that Simone read two authors who would continue to influence her throughout her life, Karl Marx and Émile Durkheim, and began her Marxist phase. In the spring of 1925—she had turned sixteen—she passed her second *bachot* with a *"mention bien,"* a superior grade. And that autumn she followed directly in her brother's footsteps by beginning to prepare for the entrance exams of the École Normale Supérieure.

By that time the emotional crisis of Simone's adolescence had provoked her to create a new persona: Between the ages of thirteen and fifteen, she evolved an appearance that would not change much for the rest of her life. A mass of uncombed black hair and huge tortoiseshell-framed glasses nearly obscured her small, delicate face. Those who met her for the first time were bound to notice the large, bold, inquisitive dark eyes that scrutinized others with an almost indiscreet curiosity. Her gestures were lively but brusque and awkward, and she was pitifully thin. Although any evidence of eating disorders was later denied by Dr. Weil to avoid the stigma then attached to anorexia, which classically sets in at puberty, her friends said that she already ate extremely little. (When parents survive a famous child by a few decades, as Dr. and Mme Weil survived Simone, a tendency to hagiography frequently occurs.) An even more forbidding aspect of her physique was the clumsy clothing with which she covered her angular body. They were the clothes of a ragtag soldier or a poor monk. Her garments were always of the same monastic, masculine cut—a cape, boyish flat-heeled shoes, a long, full skirt, and a long body-obscuring jacket in dark colors. Beyond an occasional wool beret, she never put on a hat, which in that decade was most unusual for a young woman of the upper class.

If costume tends to express our inner attitudes, Simone's getups called out that she considered it a great misfortune to have been born a woman. And in this forthright repudiation of femaleness her powerful mother was playing an important role. Having always regretted her aborted career as a medical doctor, she seems to have rechanneled her own frustrations about gender toward her daughter. "The levity, the lack of forthrightness, all these little girls' posturings and grimaces," Selma wrote a friend in those years. "I'll always prefer the good little boys, boisterous and sincere . . . and I do my best to encourage in Simone not the simpering graces of a little girl, but the forthrightness of a boy, even if this must at times seem rude."[13] In fact, both of Simone's parents seem to have encouraged her boyish attributes. They teasingly called her "Simon" and referred to her as "our son number two," and from her early adolescence their daughter had played along by often signing her letters "your respectful son." The great idol of Simone's childhood, her brother, André, may also have played a subtle role in her complex gender identity. Since she was eight or nine his affectionate nickname for her had been *"la trollesse,"* in reference to "troll," the androgynous imp of Norse mythology.

Family dynamics were not the only influence on the language of Simone's clothes. Her drab, unisex costuming was equally shaped by her visceral instinct for equality and by her increasingly radical politics. "It would be better if everyone dressed the same way and for the same amount of money," she told a friend when she was still in her teens. "That way . . . nobody would see our differences."[14] There also seems to have been some theatricality in Simone's accoutrements, as there is in most sumptuary decisions. As a budding left-wing activist who was contemptuous of bourgeois customs and, moreover, had a great sense of mischief, she didn't mind shocking some people as she made her egalitarian points concerning cheap, swift dressing. However, these deliberate aspects of Simone's cross-dressing, and her need to disfigure herself into a caricature of the beautiful girl she could have been, were related to far darker, more tragic aspects of her personality: the despair caused by her general sense of unworthiness, her sense that she was plain and somehow incomplete and could not be loved as a woman, her deep unease about issues of gender. There was only one source of strength about her identification with men: Although terrified of any sexual contact, she got along with them marvelously as "comrades," far better than with women. Throughout her life men would be her closest friends, advisers, and confidants.

One such man was Alain, the renowned teacher who was to change her life, and whom she met upon entering *cagne* at the Lycée Henri IV. He had his own singular reaction to Simone. He called her "the Martian," after H. G. Wells's interstellar dwellers, who are all eyes and brain. "She had nothing of us," he recalled, "and sovereignly judged us all."[15]

2. The Master Teacher

"ALAIN" WAS the pen name of Émile Chartier, a philosopher and prolific author who is now published in four volumes of the Pléiade (an edition limited to masters of world literature) and who fifty years after his death is still known to most lycée students in France. A gruff, plainspoken Norman who flaunted his working-class origins and shuffled about the classroom with a limp caused by a World War I injury, Alain was defiant of most forms of bourgeois sensibility: Once, when his classroom was visited by a government inspector, he went on, undaunted, instructing his students on their humanitarian obligations to prostitutes. Alain refused all earmarks of literary celebrity and shunned almost every kind of traditional comfort. He even declined marriage, stating that domesticity might diminish the energy of his writing, and only in his eighties agreed to marry the woman who had shared his life for forty years.

Alain disliked radios, telephones, politicians, and airplanes, disdained Einstein and Freud, and had no use for modern literature (with the exception of Paul Valéry). His philosophical method—what there was of it—was above all based on skepticism. Like his favorite philosopher, Descartes, Alain argued that doubt is the true agent of enlightenment, the only antidote to dogmatism and fanaticism, and enables us to grasp paradox and absurdity. He also believed that as long as we use the right methods, all human beings have far more gifts than we're given to believe, and that there does not exist a form of work for which we don't have the aptitude. The most liberating aspect of Alain's impact on Simone was his trust in this Cartesian lay wisdom. His view that any intelligence that uses the proper method can achieve the same ends as the greatest genius was bound to be a solace to anyone who had grown up, as Simone had, in the shade of an outlandishly gifted sibling.

During Simone's years at the Lycée Henri IV, Alain's lectures, offered to a *cagne* class of twenty-seven men and two women, were held three times a week, in two-hour sessions (1929 was only the second year that women were admitted to Normale, and, consequently, to any kind of preparation for it). With old-fashioned gallantry, he asked his two women students—Simone Weil and Simone Pétrement, who became a philosopher and Weil's first major biographer—to sit in the center of the front row, right beneath his blackboard. According to one of their fellow students, the lectures proceeded in the following fashion: "Alain entered the class . . . without even looking at us and would sit down with three quarters of his body, including his shoulders, turned the other way. He would brusquely write on the blackboard a Sibylline formula which served as his starting point; then, again very brusquely, he would reassert the concept with a series of extravagant word games, illustrate it with a thousand examples, overturn all possible points in opposition and let it echo in our minds."[1]

Often quoting Stendhal to the effect that one should "write every day, whether inspired or not," Alain encouraged his students to sit down at a desk and write prolifically, as he did, at least two hours a day. He maintained that one should write on large sheets of paper, in a beautiful hand, with extremely wide margins for annotations (a beautiful script was a token of self-mastery, and he trusted in the inspirational power of blank paper). Alain's students were urged to hand in essays of a few pages' length—he called them *"topoi,"* or "themes"—every three weeks, on issues of their choice. He was convinced that "learning to write well means learning to think well," and wanted his students to express universal truths in clear and simple language. Alain also believed in the importance of keeping daily company with the great minds of the past through constant rereading and memorization. His favorites were Plato, Descartes, Kant, and Spinoza, and these philosophers would have considerable influence on Simone. At the beginning of each school year, he chose two great authors to study—one a philosopher, the other a poet or novelist—and devoted an hour a week to each throughout the term. (During the three years Simone attended his class, the pairings of featured authors were Plato and Balzac, Kant and Homer, Marcus Aurelius and Lucretius.)

Although he was adamantly anticlerical and distrusted all organized religions, there was also a mystical, religious side to Alain's thought that eventually would much affect Simone. He found great sources of truth and beauty in such Christian motifs as the Crucified One, the Virgin and Child, and the saints. He spoke of them with visible admiration, so much so that he unwittingly made some converts among his students. ("He was the first man to reveal to me the greatness of Christian doctrine," André Maurois later recalled, "and induced me to accept a large part of it.") Alain went so far as to say, "Only the man who believes thinks."[2] Yet he held to the notion that true *faith,* "composed entirely of will and courage," is directly opposed to *credulity,* which commits itself to beliefs imposed by social institutions. In the tradition of socially radical Christianity, which in the millennium just past has run from Saint Francis of Assisi to Martin Luther King, Jr., and the contemporary Catholic activists Daniel and Philip Berrigan, Alain saw the divine incarnated in all those who are powerless—the very poor, the infant Christ of the creche, the adult Christ of Calvary.

What would it have been like to meet the eighteen-, nineteen-year-old Simone Weil during the years she was sitting in Alain's classroom? The beauty of her porcelain skin, of her delicate features, continued to be all but hidden by her huge glasses, her grubby clothes, her awkward gait. And those who saw through to her beauty wondered why she had chosen to make herself so ugly. She continued to be wafer thin in her late teens, and friends noted that she ate very slowly and sparingly, as if masticating food were a painful chore. She remained as averse to physical contact as she had been in childhood, shunning even the most casual of hugs or comradely linking of elbows (her dread of sexuality seems to have been deepened in early adolescence by the sight of an exhibitionist in the Luxembourg Gardens, an episode her brother alludes to in his memoirs and to which she later refers, just once, in her journals).

As for her manner, she retained the argumentative, eccentric style she had evolved in her mid-teens, and which had become even more intransigent. Eager to enjoy intense friendships, she undermined that social impulse through imperious critical pronouncements that often isolated her from others. She chose her friends impetuously, provoking them with the tenacity of her questions. But when she saw an unfavorable trait in one of them, she was capable of brusquely ending the friendship. Her more admiring schoolmates described her as "amazingly all of a piece," tolerating no discrepancy between people's beliefs and their way of life. "What I can not stand is *compromise*," she used to say about people who did not live in accordance with their beliefs. She accompanied this judgment with a horizontal, violent cutting gesture of her hand, which she repeated whenever she was breaking off contact with someone who did not fulfill her very demanding standards of conduct. "Even though I loved her, I always sensed that a serene friendship with her was impossible," said Camille Marcoux, a very close friend. "[There was] the rudeness and rawness of her manners, her unusual appearance and, above all, the battering of those ruthless judgments." Many of Simone's friends testify to her aggressively contentious streak. "All around her there was turmoil [and] confusion," said another friend, Clémence Ramnoux. "She always had to be involving you in demonstrations, urging you to get signatures, sending you out with leaflets. I withdrew."[3]

Pétrement portrays a far more vulnerable Simone. "I can still see her," she writes, "crouched over her note paper, her fingers often covered with ink stains, writing very slowly and painfully, quick to turn her head, attentive to everything, observing things ardently from behind her thick glasses."[4] When other students talked, Simone listened intently, neck craned, drawing little figures on her paper—fantastic creatures, curiously resembling cabalistic drawings. The doodling seemed to relax her from the excruciating effort of taking notes on her professors' lectures: Because of the slowness with which she wrote, Simone often had to borrow her friends' notes, especially in Alain's classes, to complete hers. Her clothes were frequently ink-splotched from the improperly closed bottle of Waterman's she always kept in her pocket, along with bulging pouches of tobacco and cigarette papers. Out on the street she put herself and anyone accompanying her at constant risk, talking and gesticulating as she walked through traffic with long, jerky steps, totally heedless of cars and escaping them by sheer chance (she claimed that a charm protected her from accidents).

Besides Simone Pétrement, Simone's closest friends at *cagne* were three men, René Château, Jacques Ganuchaud, and Pierre Letellier. Simone sat at a bistro on the Rue des Canettes for hours on end with her three comrades, talking, drinking black coffee, and chain-smoking her hand-rolled cigarettes (she tried wine a few times to be "one of the boys," but could only drink tiny amounts without getting sick). The friends' talkfests concentrated on philosophy, politics, and, inevitably, Alain's teaching methods, for as graduates of the École Normale they would all have to put in some years as lycée professors. How would they fulfill, in their own teaching careers, Alain's high-minded view of education, which was to turn schools into "centers of humanity" that could fight against prejudices, violence, and injustice? The conversations sometimes lasted until the bistro closed down at 2 A.M., and occasionally the friends moved on and saw dawn come up at a café in the Halles market.

Although Simone, like Alain, never became a member of the Communist Party, in her late teens she was clearly more attracted to it than to any other political group. At *cagne* and Normale she would often draw the hammer and sickle on her rough drafts and notes. The Party paper, *L'Humanité*, remained her bible for some years, and for a while she spent Sunday mornings selling it in front of Sacré-Coeur for two aged, impoverished newsvendors who were too infirm to leave their homes. Her brother reported seeing, on her desk, the unfinished draft of a letter requesting membership in the Party. It began with the words: "Moved by profound feelings of solidarity . . ." But she never mailed it. Her rebellious, individualistic nature was totally unfit for the Communist Party, and within two years of finishing Normale she would be denouncing the Party as an even greater enemy than capitalism.

Some classmates, referring to Simone's beloved Kant, called her "the Categorical Imperative in skirts" because of her need to draw all ideas to their ultimate logical conclusion. And yet she had so many redeeming graces. Totally ingenuous, she was capable of bursting out with such naïvetés as "I wish that my parents had been poor!"[5] Her indomitable sense of justice was accompanied by a black, ironic sense of humor. Every week she walked about the halls of Normale bursting into great gales of laughter as she read some political satire in the left-wing *Le Canard Enchaîné.* And her feelings of inadequacy led her to acquire an admirable will to self-mastery. This had been a cardinal point of Alain's teaching, and she may well have put it into practice more obsessively than any other student he ever had. When, for instance, he chided her for her sloppy, scrawled handwriting and suggested that she try to write more legibly, Simone, aged sixteen, set out to reform her script totally. First she worked several hours a day in a child's composition book to form beautiful single letters, using matchsticks to make her verticals straighter; later she concentrated on linking the letters into perfectly formed words. Within a few months she had forced her awkward hands to achieve a perpendicular, handsomely constructed script.

In Simone this cult of self-mastery could all too readily become self-destructive, however. Setting out to correct her extreme ineptness in sports, for instance, she joined the first women's rugby team in France, founded at the Femina athletic club in Paris. She inevitably returned from the playing field covered with mud and bruises, and often sat in the wet grass after the games, brooding about her blunders and her awkwardness. According to her mother, this was the way she contracted the larval sinusitis that vastly exacerbated her headaches and would plague her for most of her life. There were more alarming signs of this impulse to extreme self-domination, which is now recognized as another frequent symptom of anorexia. For a long time her classmates at *cagne* noticed a round, deep wound, like a burn, on the back of her left hand, which took many months to heal. She refused to tell her friends what had caused it. But it was widely believed that she had held a cigarette to her hand during one of her long nights of work, either to test her capacity for pain or to punish herself for some personal shortcoming that most other people would have made light of.

Simone's insistence on practicing the politics she preached was equally awesome, particularly for a spoiled upper-class teenager. There had been much talk among Simone and her friends of reviving the "people's universities," popular before the Great War, at which blue-collar workers would receive grounding in cultural subjects. And this project struck Simone as ideal. Along with her two friends Ganuchaud and Château, she founded an association called the Social Education Group, which offered evening classes in mathematics, physics, sociology, and political economy to railroad workers, preparing them to take exams for higher-paying clerical posts. By 1928, the year she entered Normale, Simone was teaching there several evenings a week. Pleased that a good number of her students succeeded in the competitive examinations for clerical jobs, she continued to teach there until 1931, when, after graduating from Normale, she left to teach in the provinces. How did the workers take to her as an instructor? While liking Simone enormously as a *"bonne camarade,"* many of them reported that they did not always grasp her farfetched and paradoxical ideas.

The support offered by Alain in the flowering of Simone's political sensibility cannot be overemphasized. He may have been the only person outside her immediate family who saw through her gauche, occasionally rude manners, her slothful attire. He admired her extraordinarily acute social conscience, and encouraged her to be faithful to her beliefs. He was also the first to encourage her to be a writer, and invited her to contribute articles to his review, *Libre Propos,* which published her very first essays. When she returned as a full-fledged Normale student to hear his lectures, he could think of no greater reward to offer the star of his incoming class, the future Gaullist leader and government minister Maurice Schumann, than to let him sit next to Simone Weil (Schumann would subsequently become one of her closest friends). Alain's central convictions would become equally pivotal to her thought: an unstinting intellectual responsibility to the world; a gospel of social action; and, above all, a passionate belief in the spiritual potential of manual labor. Work, Alain believed, manifests the mind's most genuine freedom. Through labor, the mind, using the body as pincers with which to grasp matter, realizes its own liberty and, simultaneously, the inadequacy of its own ideas. It is this symbiotic collaboration of mind and body that turns work into "a sacrament of life." The very variety of topics Weil grappled with throughout her career—from folklore to the growth of political parties, from scientific theorems to theological reflections—also mirrors her teacher's remarkable breadth of concerns.

Of the papers that Simone wrote for Alain during her years in *cagne,* two are particularly significant. One, written in her first months with him, is a commentary on a tale of Jacob Grimm's, "The Six Swans." Six brothers—so the tale goes—were transformed into swans by their stepmother, a witch. In order to enable them to regain human form, their sister spent six years sewing six shirts made of white anemones; until she finished her task she had to keep an oath of total silence, which posed constant dangers because she could not defend herself against her stepmother's unjust accusations. As she was about to be put to death, six swans—her brothers—swooped toward her from the sky. She threw the shirts onto them, and they regained their human form and saved their sister. Simone commented on this story in this fashion:

> Acting is never difficult; we always do too much and waste ourselves in disorderly actions. Making six shirts of anemones and being silent: that is our only way of acquiring power. . . . [I]t is almost impossible to sew anemones together and turn them into a shirt, and the difficulty is such that it prevents any additional action that would alter the purity of that six-year silence. In this world purity is the only force . . . it is a fragment of

truth. . . . Refraining from action: here lies our only force and our only virtue.[6]

Alain gave Simone's paper an "Excellent," in the French grading system the equivalent of our A+. Another of her *cagne* essays he thought of highly deals with an episode in the life of Alexander the Great. In order to show solidarity with his men by sharing their thirst, Alexander, while crossing the desert, had poured out on the ground the helmetful of water his soldiers had brought him. Simone observes that Alexander's act only safeguarded his own purity and humanity, and was not useful to anyone else. The true moral of the story, she pointed out, is the following:

> Alexander's well-being, if he had drunk the water, would have separated him from his soldiers. . . . Everything takes place in Alexander's soul . . . so it suffices to be just and pure to save the world, an idea expressed by the myth of the Man-God who redeemed the sins of men by justice alone. . . . Sacrifice is the acceptance of pain, the refusal to obey the animal in oneself, and the will to redeem suffering men through voluntary suffering. Every saint has poured out the water; every saint has rejected all well-being that would separate him from the suffering of men.[7]

She was only sixteen when she wrote those words, which foreshadow her entire spiritual development.

There was as much mischief in Simone as there was spirituality and combative zeal. While at *cagne* she derived great amusement from coming to blows with a school official while protesting his decision that male and female students must sit in separate areas of the classrooms. She was also delighted to be suspended for eight days for smoking in the men's courtyard (smoking was not allowed in the building, and all the courtyards were reserved for men). However, the unruliness she flaunted could occasionally harm her study patterns. She lavished such energy and attention on her philosophy course with Alain that she neglected a few others. In June 1927, after two years of *cagne*, she was turned down in her entrance exams for Normale because of a low grade in history, a discipline Alain tended to deride. "An intelligent young girl who evidently feels that she is *above* history," was how the professor grading the exam described her.[8] That was a hard censure for a Weil to swallow, and she immediately started reforming her ways. She spent part of the year in total seclusion in the country, with a friend of her parents who ran a girls' tutoring school near Bordeaux. Needless to say the other girls, staring at her strange gait and tobacco-stuffed pockets, considered her a very odd character; but she was indifferent to them, relished her seclusion, and stayed up into the dawn hours studying her history. (She did make friends with the gardener, however, and flouted convention by inviting him to her room to discuss politics, urging him, of course, to unionize.)

Simone's self-imposed withdrawal paid off: In the spring of 1928 she was accepted at Normale with the highest national ranking of that year's applicants.

Alain wrote evaluations of Simone Weil's work every trimester for a period of three years. His appraisals chronicle the progress of her intellectual growth; they also offer insights into the demanding standards the exemplary French professor of the prewar era imposed on his students:

For the first trimester of the year 1925–26: "She is cogent and lucid, and shows frequent wit and distinction in her powers of analysis. Her overall perspectives are less clear; she has to learn how to construct a coherent argument. But she already shows an intuitive mind and much may be expected of her."

For the second trimester: "Excellent student, who learns, disciplines herself, and develops with admirable rapidity and assurance. Her style lags a trifle behind her ideas, but one can predict brilliant results that may well prove astonishing."

For the first trimester of the year 1926–27: "Very fine student, greatly gifted, who, should, however, be on guard against over-abstruse reflections expressed in almost impenetrable language."

For the third trimester of 1927–28, her last official term with Alain: "Unusual strength of mind, broad culture. She will succeed brilliantly if she does not go down obscure paths. In any event, she will certainly be noticed."[9]

There is also the appreciation he would offer her six years later, in 1935, when she sent him the text of her pivotal essay *Oppression and Liberty:*

> Your example will inspire courage in generations deluded by ontology and ideology. . . . I am sure that works of this sort . . . serious and rigorous . . . are the only ones that will open the future and true Revolution. . . . [T]he sole thing that could prevent you from fulfilling your mission is indignation. Keep in mind what I have always said: whatever is misanthropic is false. . . . Fraternally, Alain.[10]

3. "Normale"

ONE OF THE MOST striking portraits of Simone Weil in her late teens is offered by Simone de Beauvoir, who had long wanted to meet her because she'd heard that Weil had broken into sobs at the news of a famine in China. She finally encountered Weil in a courtyard of the Sorbonne.

"I envied a heart able to beat across the world," Beauvoir wrote in *Memoirs of a Dutiful Daughter*.

> She intrigued me because of her great reputation for intelligence and her bizarre outfits. . . . I managed to get near her one day. I don't know how the conversation got started. She said in piercing tones that only one thing mattered these days: the revolution that would feed all the starving people on the earth. I retorted, no less adamantly, that the problem was not to make men happy, but to help them find a meaning in their existence. She glared at me and said, "It's clear you've never gone hungry." Our relations ended right there. I realized that she had classified me as a high-minded little bourgeoise, and I was angry.[1]

But Simone Weil would not have to contend with Beauvoir, who was studying for a doctorate in literature at the Sorbonne. Taken into Normale with a group of twenty-nine men in 1928, Weil was the only woman in her class (this was one of the first years women were fully admitted to the institution). Three women, her friend Simone Pétrement among them, had entered Normale the previous fall, and the administration had assigned this tiny group a "den" of its own on the ground floor. The establishment, which had been founded under Napoleon to train teachers for government lycées, is not a "school" in our current meaning of the word but an academy of sorts, which involves a number of privileges and obligations. Headquartered on the Rue d'Ulm, a few hundred yards from the Sorbonne, it is separated from the French university system, which is open to all lycée graduates, by its fiercely selective entrance exams. In exchange for the privilege of a government scholarship and, if they need it, room and board, *Normaliens,* upon fulfilling all requirements for their *agrégations* or graduate degrees, sign a contract promising to teach in the lycée system for ten years. Most of the course work at Normale is done at the Sorbonne, but in Simone's time, as in ours, even attendance at the Sorbonne lectures was optional: Those who wanted to study on their own could do so, for Normale's only requirements for graduation are that students write a number of theses and earn the "licenses" required to teach in government lycées by passing a series of exams.

Because of the institution's eminence as the training ground for France's intellectual elite, it has long been a *Normalien* tradition to disdain Sorbonne professors, and generally to display an air of insolence and superiority. So it was natural that Simone attended no Sorbonne courses to speak of and preferred to continue her training in philosophy by auditing Alain's lectures at Henri IV. Moreover, she was never tactful toward those in positions of power, and was noted for her frequent clashes with Normale's authorities. One of her bêtes noires was the sociologist Celestin Bouglé, the director of studies. In her first year at the school, during a meeting at which Bouglé gave the students a pep talk on the subject of patriotism, Simone stood up and read, in a spirit of cutting irony, a 1912 speech by the statesman Raymond Poincaré stating that France might have to invade Belgium for reasons of national defense (it was Germany's 1914 invasion of that country that had triggered World War I). "When she had finished, there was a moment of silence," writes Jacques Cabaud, a *Normalien* who attended the meeting. "Bouglé, unnerved, took out his watch and said, 'Twelve o'clock, time for lunch.'"[2] The phrase "Twelve o'clock, time for lunch" quickly became a catchword among the students, who repeated it, with flourishing gestures imitating Bouglé's, whenever they couldn't find an answer to a disconcerting question. Simone kept needling Bouglé on many other issues throughout her years at Normale. On one occasion she asked him for a contribution for the unemployed. He gave her twenty francs but warned her that his gift must remain anonymous. Whereupon she immediately put up a sign on the school's bulletin board that said: "Follow the example of your Director of Studies, become an anonymous donor to the unemployment benefit fund." From then on Bouglé called her "the Red Virgin" and criticized her on every possible occasion.

Simone's home life continued to be as serene as her student life was agitated. In May 1929, the spring of her first year at Normale, her family moved apartments for the first time since the end of the Great War. Their beautiful new flat, on the sixth and seventh floors of a recently finished building on the Rue Auguste Comte, looked out directly on the Luxembourg Gardens. (The top floor was originally reserved for André, but since he was away on teaching stints much of the year it often served as a guest suite for one or another of Simone's large collection of radical friends.) Situated in a hilly section of town, the Montagne Sainte-Geneviève, the Weils' new home enjoyed a broad view that included vistas of the Eiffel Tower, the dome of the Invalides, the top of the Arc de Triomphe, the roofs of the Opéra and the Louvre, the steeple of Sainte-Chapelle, and the dome of the Pantheon. Dr. and Mme Weil would live in the apartment until 1940, reclaim it when they returned to Paris after the war, and remain in it until their deaths in 1955 and 1965 respectively. André Weil's own family, in fact, sold the flat on the Rue Auguste Comte only in the late 1990s.

The spring her family moved to this new home, Simone's maternal grandmother, Mme Reinherz, who had strongly disapproved of her granddaughter's radical views, died of cancer at the age of seventy-nine. In the last months Simone made great efforts to be reconciled with her grandmother; she found friends to play the piano for Mme Reinherz, and she read *Les Misérables* aloud to her; the two had long conversations that seemed to calm the old lady. Mme Weil believed that Simone helped her grandmother to accept death.

In summers, at vacation time, Simone spent increasingly less time with her parents, finding every occasion she could to do manual labor. One year she went to stay with a maternal aunt in the Jura, where she worked as a farmhand for ten hours a day, digging potatoes. For two summers in the late 1920s she also spent the harvest months in Normandy at the home of her friend Pierre Letellier, displaying a frenetic energy when she worked the harvest with his family. The thistles collected by the reapers were piled in tall heaps after being separated from the wheat. Upon being told by young Letellier that men were coming to pick them up with prongs, Simone insisted on picking sheaves bigger than herself with her bare arms, saying, "Why the men, and not me?" In the evening she asked the same question when the farmhands tried to stop her from unloading the wheat-laden carts; she insisted on working at the same rate as her male peers.

An even more dramatic instance of Simone's attempts to do "men's work" was her stint as a fisherman on the Normandy Coast, where she vacationed with her parents in 1931, at the end of her last year at Normale. Dr. and Mme Weil, sensing her emotional need for this kind of exertion, had gone to Normandy ahead of her to help her join a fishing group. Most of the seamen were reluctant to take on an inexperienced woman, but one fisherman, Marcel Lecarpentier, owner of a four-man boat, acceded to Dr. Weil's request.

"I decided to please Dr. Weil when I saw his daughter running along the shore like a madwoman," he recalls. "She was going into the sea in her wide skirts; she was getting soaking wet, without a slicker. I'd already left shore but I turned around and went back and picked her up. I borrowed a set of oilskins to wrap her in . . . she had a little book and a pencil with her; she spent a good part of the nights drawing the constellations and writing."

Lecarpentier eventually welcomed Simone into his house, became a friend, and left a long recollection of her:

> She wasn't pretty and she wouldn't take care of herself. She was a real ragamuffin. Her parents suffered from this . . . and someone else in my village . . . kept telling me, "Don't have her come to your house. She's a Commu-

nist and will bring you trouble." I didn't mind at all; she had a right to my table. . . . Moreover she wasn't a Communist. She used to teach my child Catechism.

When the sea was too rough to go out, Simone helped Lecarpentier continue his own education in arithmetic and French literature, and went on tutoring him long after she went back to Paris. "For months to come . . . I would send her my notebooks and she would correct them and send them back to me," Lecarpentier recalled.

And she continued to send me books . . . *Gold Seekers of Alaska*, for example. . . . She wanted to know our misery. She wanted to free the worker. This was the goal of her life. I would say to her, "But you're the daughter of rich people." She'd say "That's my misfortune, I wish my parents had been poor." "You wouldn't know so much, you wouldn't have studied so much," I'd tell her. "No, no, you and I would have gotten to the same point," she'd answer.

Lecarpentier's testimony emphasizes Simone's total neglect of physical comfort, her concern for the penury of most working families, and her keen attention to the financial details of labor.

Despite her family's wealth she hated clothes and jewelry, she would glide, glide above what people thought of her. She loved solitude and the sea. She always had a headache; they'd come on her like waves of emptiness. Another time she really frightened me. . . . There was a terrible storm and I asked her to tie herself down; she refused. "I'm ready to die," she said, "I've always done my duty."

"She followed our work as if through a microscope," he also recalled. "She watched the price of fish and calculated the proper divisions. 'Why don't you form a cooperative, Marcel,' she suggested. . . . She used to ask me all the time if there were any families that needed aid; I didn't tell her, because I didn't want her to become penniless."[3]

All this time, as she tried different kinds of physical labor, Simone was deepening the mystique of work she'd evolved as Alain's student. She believed that work is the truest road to self-knowledge, and that it supplies the only valid form of social cohesion. For in her view, most other bonds—family ties, the affection of lovers, even the religion that links fellow worshipers—are nourished by destructive emotions, by "the same seductive accord that engenders all wars." Work, however, unifies in the purest way: "Religion makes love manifest, but work . . . creates respect for the human person, and equality; that is why collaboration [in work] creates enduring friendships for which there is no substitute."[4] This proto-Marxist view of work hinged on an admittedly naïve idealization—if not canonization—of the proletariat, which she saw as a form of contemporary sainthood. On the basis of having taught Plato and Descartes to railroad workers at evening school, Simone earnestly believed that a member of the working class, if given the proper study guidance, could reach the truth far better than the average intellectual. Sitting on the subway next to Simone Pétrement one day, she pointed to a man in his factory overalls, and said, "You see, it's not just in a spirit of justice that I love them. I love them naturally, because I find them far more beautiful than the bourgeois."[5]

...

At the École Normale, Simone continued to be looked on as a troublesome tomboy, intimidating and thoroughly tactless but admirable in her determination and ideals. Fellow students tried to avoid her in the corridors because of "the blunt, thoughtless way she had of confronting you with your responsibilities by asking for your signature on a petition . . . or a contribution for some trade union strike fund,"[6] said her classmate Camille Marcoux, another ardent follower of Alain.

Simone had met Marcoux in one of their first weeks at Normale, when, after approving of something he had said during a student meeting, she accosted him abruptly in the men's dining room, "Are you Marcoux? Follow me." There ensued years of long walks and endless conversations in cafés, of jointly taught courses at the railroad workers' education center she had helped to start, where they both struck up a friendship with the founder of the school, Alain's friend Lucien Cancouët. They often went to dinner with Cancouët and his wife in their tiny two-room apartment, and there were occasions when Marcoux was struck by Simone's total obliviousness to "normal" boy-girl relationships. "Cancouët thought we were something other than friends," Marcoux recalled. "He would look at us in a suggestive manner. I was embarrassed; Simone never even noticed it."[7] Marcoux also testified to Simone's continuing intransigence and the ruthless manner in which she could cut off friends who in some small way displeased her. He once suffered such an estrangement from her because he used a text by Bouglé, the economist and Normale administrator whom Simone particularly loathed, while making a presentation on the nineteenth-century socialist reformer Pierre-Joseph Proudhon. "She castigated me ferociously at the end of the presentation," he recalled. "Later, she told my comrades that for her I was 'dead.'" Mme Weil continued to invite Marcoux to play the piano with her and stay for dinner afterward, but for some time Simone refused to even look at him. "She would take her place at the table without a greeting and would leave before the end of the meal,"[8] Marcoux commented. It took more than a year for Simone to reconcile with him.

Marcoux also recalled Simone's exceptional powers of concentration, which could be highly detrimental to her health—she could continue to study for days on end without food or sleep. When there were any texts she wished to reflect on with particular intensity, she used to study them on her knees, the volumes spread out on the floor before her, crawling from volume to volume, from one end of the room to the other, oblivious to the rest of her surroundings. To study her geometry—a particularly beloved subject—she used to go to a bank of the Seine, near a pillar of the Austerlitz bridge, where barges unloaded large blocks of stone. She had a special attraction to those stones, which she associated with geometric shapes. Whenever Marcoux came to meet her, she would be kneeling on the pavement of the quay, the world shut out, immersed in the book before her, occasionally tugging at a lock of her hair.

In her last year at Normale, in preparation for her final exams there, Simone had set herself a formidable program of work. In the field of moral philosophy alone, for instance, she made the following list of obligatory readings:

> To study thoroughly: Aristotle, Bentham, Schopenhauer, and Nietzsche.
> To brush up on: the Stoics, Epicureans, Skeptics (Mon-

taigne), and Descartes, Pascal, Rousseau, Proudhon, Comte . . . Marx, and Tolstoy.

To review carefully: Machiavelli, Hobbes, Leibnitz . . . Bergson, Schelling, Fichte, Hegel, and Lenin.

To review quickly: Plotinus, the Middle Ages, Bacon (?), Malebranche, Voltaire, and the Encyclopedists.

To study systematically: the pre-Socratics, the Sophists, Socrates, Plato, Locke, Hume, Berkeley, Spinoza, Kant.[9]

As the topic of her final dissertation at Normale—one of the several requirements toward obtaining a diploma, or *agrégation*, to teach in lycées and universities—Simone chose the theme "Science and Perception in Descartes." Her essay is best described as a rethinking of Descartes's *Discourse on Method* in the more personal, contemplative style of his *Meditations*, with a strong emphasis on self-mastery. But the formulas she employs are a little different from Descartes's and show the influence of Alain's emphasis on pure will. In Weil's essay, Descartes's *cogito* takes the form "I *can*, therefore I am." "From the moment that I act, I make myself exist. . . . What I am is defined by what I can do."

This early period of Weil's writing already reveals the terse, paradoxical style of her later work. Her epigrams recall, in turn, the enigmatic abruptness of Zen aphorisms ("Void is the only plenitude") and the cryptic economy of Pascal's *Pensées*, which seems to have influenced her more deeply than any other French classic.

I must be devious, cunning, I must set myself obstacles that lead me to where I want to go. . . .[10]

God is proven in some way by the extreme difficulty of believing in him. . . .[11]

The good is . . . the motion by which we break away from ourselves as individuals . . . to affirm ourselves as true men, that is, as sharers in God. . . .

God is proven and posited by right action, and in no other way. . . . One must deserve to believe in God.[12]

So the twenty-one-year-old Simone was still very influenced by Kant: To believe in God is mostly to act correctly. Although she was extremely interested in religious issues, and passionately defended, in arguments with her agnostic friends, the genuineness of Pascal's mystical conversion ("Enter my heart . . . to endure through me what remains of your Passion,"[13] she quotes from a prayer of Pascal's in one of her school papers), she continued to identify religion closely with morality. The possibility of contact with a personal God still seemed very remote to her, and in her view the existence of God could neither be affirmed nor denied.

As her thesis mentor at Normale, Simone had chosen the highly influential philosopher Léon Brunschvicg, France's leading authority on Pascal, whose edition of the *Pensées* remains unsurpassed to our day. Her choice of mentor offers further insight into her affinity for Pascal—it was typical of her aggressive side to adopt a historic role model whom she both admired and criticized, with whom she could often argue. While intensely disliking Pascal's theology, she shared with him an obsession with issues of justice, a powerful ascetic streak, and a deep distrust of power and of all forms of nationalism. Her attitude toward the real-life mentor she had chosen—the highly conservative Brunschvicg, whom she both esteemed and derided—was equally confrontational: She greatly offended him, throughout her four years at Normale, by never once consulting him while she was working on the very thesis he was supposed to direct. Like Bouglé, Brunschvicg had distrusted Simone from the start for being a follower of Alain's, whose oddly radical ideas he detested. He gave her thesis on Descartes 10 out of 20 points, the lowest grade a student could earn without flunking.

Normale, like the Sorbonne, also required written and oral exams for the *agrégation.* In 1931, Simone's graduation year, the two topics for the written exam in the field of philosophy were "Causality in Hume," and the following motif: "Must moral judgment deal with act, intention, or character?" As for the orals, Simone's subject was "the beautiful in nature and art," and several of her classmates gathered to attend this session, for which she received an outstanding grade of 19 out of 20. However, due to Brunschvicg's hostility to her written dissertation, Simone only received a middle ranking in her overall grades. Out of 11 students granted diplomas in a class of 107—this low percentage was not unusual, for only a small fraction of *Normaliens* ever pass its harrowing series of exams—she graduated seventh, a ranking that disappointed her.

While predicting how that year's crop of students would fare in their exams, Simone's bête noire, director of studies Bouglé, was reported to have said about Simone: "As for the Red Virgin, we'll leave her in peace to make bombs for the coming revolution." He had another caustic comment about her. When his graduates were being interviewed by the Ministry of Education, which traditionally queried *Normaliens* about which regions of France they would prefer to work in as teachers, Bouglé had a future all set for Simone: "We'll send the Red Virgin as far away as possible so that we'll never hear of her again," he said to one of her fellow students.

Actually, at graduation time Simone was not quite sure whether she wanted to teach in the lycée system at all, for she was flirting with the notion of going to work in a factory. But the economic crisis was so severe—the tail end of the Great Depression struck France particularly hard in 1931—that she decided to postpone her plans for factory work. So she did not write to the Ministry of Education until midsummer, and requested a teaching post "preferably in a port (Le Havre, if possible) or in an industrial town in northern France." Instead of that she was assigned to the other end of the country, as Bouglé would have wished, to the town of Le Puy, seventy miles southwest of Lyons and nine hours by train away from Paris. The location appalled her. She tried to lobby against this appointment with the help of a member of the Chamber of Deputies, but the Ministry of Education refused to change it. An *agrégée,* it replied, does not "have the right to choose her post, or to annul an appointment in favor of the post that she desires."[14]

Mme Weil and her "Simonette" left for Le Puy at the end of September. A picturesque town of fifteen thousand inhabitants, it is famous for its manufacture of lace, its beautiful Romanesque church, and its huge bronze statue of the Virgin Mary. One of the first things that crossed Simone's eye as she walked through town was a postcard of that statue, which is set on a huge cliff and is called "the Red Virgin of Le Puy." She sent it to Bouglé.

PART II: COMMUNITY

Simone in uniform at the time of her participation
in the Spanish Civil War, summer 1936

4. The Militant Years, 1931–34

FOR THE NEXT FEW years of Simone's teaching career Mme Weil traveled with her daughter to whatever town she was assigned, found apartments for her, stocked her larder on her monthly visits, and generally tried to keep her from undermining her health. At Le Puy, she even accompanied Simone to her appointment with the headmistress, an occasion that made Simone so nervous that she put on a hat and white gloves. She was such a young-looking twenty-two that on the day she came to call on the headmistress, the porter of the lycée, mistaking her for a student, asked her which classes she'd come to sign up for. After calling on "Madame la Directrice," Mme Weil and Simone started looking for an apartment. Le Puy's living conditions were relatively primitive, and Mme Weil soon found Simone one of the few flats in town that had a bathroom. It was far too large to live in alone, some five rooms, and even though she coaxed a fellow teacher of Simone's at the lycée to share it, Mme Weil needed all her diplomatic skills to persuade her daughter to live there. Simone particularly detested the idea of having a living room and soon turned it into a large closet, filling it with ropes on which the two women were to hang their clothes and laundry. Mme Weil also found a maid for them whom Simone insisted on paying skilled workers' union rates, five francs an hour, instead of the two francs normally given to domestic help. Even the maid protested the high fee, fearing she was being involved in dishonest dealings, and to make up for her grand salary she brought huge bags of pinecones for kindling.

But instead of making fires Simone persuaded her housemate, another student of Alain's, named Simone Anthériou, to use the bags of pinecones as seats. She had decided not to heat the apartment out of sympathy for the unemployed who could not afford heating fuel. (She would be surprised to learn that most of them lived in well-heated spaces.) Her mother would have additional causes for worry: Her Simonette was showing signs of increasingly serious eating problems. Mlle Anthériou soon observed that meals had become a terrible chore for her housemate; she only accepted very fresh food of the highest quality—a blemish on a pear made her stop eating. The problem was aggravated whenever her migraines plagued her; on those occasions she often vomited and could not bear to consume anything but raw grated potatoes. (It's worth noting that Simone's anorexic symptoms, which her father never admitted, began to be chronicled by her friends as soon as she left home.) Mme Weil sent the women huge packages of food and constantly invented ruses to protect her child's health, even giving money to the other Simone, on the sly, to buy the best cuts of meat. The young women's domestic skills were clearly close to nil: "Do you eat bacon raw or cooked?" Simone asked her mother in one of her letters home. "The place is freezing, no heating, and it's been 3 or 4 below zero for several days," Mme Weil soon complained in a letter to her son, André, who was teaching at a university in India. "I couldn't get mad with the poor troll, who's so good and affectionate to me. . . . [I]n the evening she eats nothing but potatoes or cocoa with water. . . . And the disorder!"[1] "No, truly, she's unmarriageable!" she exclaimed in another note to her son. And Mme Weil often made the tiring nine-hour trip from Paris to Le Puy, saying that *she* was the one on whom Bouglé, Simone's oppressor at Normale, had played a bad trick.

Simone had fifteen girls in her philosophy class at Le Puy, and also gave courses in Greek and in art history. At first the students were amused by her awkwardness, her clumsy way of holding chalk, the total anarchy of her clothes. But within a few weeks they came to admire her deeply and tried to protect her from her own clumsiness, helping her to change her sweaters, for instance, which she often put on inside out. They were impressed by the way she returned their papers overnight, beautifully corrected though often pocked with cigarette burns; by the thoughtfulness with which she visited the dormitories on holidays to chat with the lonely boarding students; by the unstinting patience and generosity with which she tutored those weak in Latin. With her threadbare vestments and her naked sandaled feet, she reminded them of some medieval hermit, and they called her "La Simone" or "Mother Weil." They found her so inspiring that when she created an optional course on the history of science, they all attended it. Her halo of voluntary poverty, the ascetic disarray of her life, touched them deeply. "The clumsiness of her gestures, above all of her hands," so one student remembers her, "her piercing look through the thick glasses, her smile—everything about her emanated a feeling of total frankness and forgetfulness of self, revealing a nobility of soul that was certainly at the root of the emotions she inspired in us."[2] There were other aspects of Simone's life they would have admired if they'd known about them. She considered her salary an intolerable privilege—the lycée professors who were Normale graduates received the highest teaching wages in the country—and kept only as much as a *non-agrégée* beginning teacher would have earned, giving the rest to a fund for the unemployed.

Simone had joined the workforce at a time when France was in very dire straits. The giddy fictions of the Jazz Age—delusions of prosperity, peace, and progress—had given way, by 1931, to a sense of stagnation and growing anxiety. There was increasing unrest among the peasantry and industrial workers, and the bourgeoisie seemed more than ever resistant to any innovation. France's swift turnover of governments was just one symptom of its instability: Between 1919 and 1940 the country would be ruled by forty-two governments, with an average life span of six months each. When the Great Depression struck Wall Street in 1929, France's governing classes, still basking in dreams of prosperity, had believed that their country would be totally impervious to the American disaster. The crash that hit France two years later, following the devaluation of the British pound in September 1931, had a catastrophic effect. Within a few months—the very autumn Simone started teaching in the lycée system—industrial production declined by 80 percent, and unemployment rose to 20 percent. Extremist right-wing movements flickered in the rural regions, and wildcat factory strikes spearheaded by Communists continually disrupted production. In the ensuing two years, the rise of Nazism in Germany and the growing evidence of totalitarianism in Soviet Russia would confront French leaders with the need for a vastly revised foreign policy.

As for the progressive young intellectuals of Simone's milieu, by 1931 they were deeply imbued with the visceral pacifism traditional to Europe's left-wing movements. They expressed equal revulsion for traditional parliamentary politics and for uncurbed capitalism, which they held responsible for the crash of 1929. The immense popularity of Charlie Chaplin's *Modern Times* in Simone's circles reflects their censure of the West's frenetic, dehumanizing industrial ethos. But their critique went further. It took the form of a general rebellion against most forms of materialism and rationalism, an anxious search for new modes of moral and spiritual renewal, and a determination to safeguard themselves against the increasingly impersonal structures of government power.

Simone assimilated many, though not all, of these intellectual currents. She militantly shared her peers' critique of capitalism as wasteful and oppressive, their rejection of the industrial ethos, their impassioned support of the trade union struggle, their enthusiasm for radical, even utopian solutions, their negative view of the Third Republic's political institutions. Yet she was far more pessimistic than most of her contemporaries; she was persuaded that Europe would soon be mired in another global conflict even more destructive than World War I. She also broke with most of her peers by categorically refusing any form of nihilism, remaining a rationalist and retaining her faith in the ability of the human mind to obtain objective knowledge. Moreover, whereas intellectuals of her generation tended to sympathize with Communism, by the time she had finished Normale, Simone had grown implacable in her hatred of the Party bureaucracy. Finally, unlike most *Normaliens*, she greatly distrusted intellectuals—her own class. She still believed, with Marx, that the proletariat could not be liberated until all hierarchical distinctions between intellectual and manual labor were abolished.

So it is understandable that at this point in her life, Simone's political sympathies lay solidly with Revolutionary Syndicalism, a political grouping named after the French word for trade union, *syndicat*. Revolutionary Syndicalism was an essentially anarchistic movement that shunned parliamentary party politics, advocated direct action by the working class, such as general strikes, and strived to establish a social order based on workers' production units (in the syndicalists' view, only unions, not political parties, could form the basis of a society in which workers would not be exploited). Greatly influenced by the teachings of Proudhon, Revolutionary Syndicalism had grown out of the strong anarchist and antiparliamentary traditions of the French working class. It was the backbone of the powerful trade union movement that blossomed at the end of the nineteenth century, when France's first major trade union, the Confédération Générale du Travail (CGT), was founded. It dominated the ideology of the CGT until the end of World War I, when the CGT's more radical members, many of them seduced by Communism, formed a rival union, the Confédération Générale du Travail Unitaire (CGTU). Although they had played a major role in founding the French Communist Party in the years immediately following the Bolshevik Revolution, by 1924 most Revolutionary Syndicalists had left the Party or been expelled, and had become a small, independent left-wing group very hostile to Communism.

By the late 1920s, when Simone began to work as a trade unionist, the CGT continued to remain aloof from all political parties; the CGTU remained closely tied to the Communist Party. By 1931 many left-wing activists, Simone among them, became dedicated to the notion that the two groups should be reunited. Upon becoming a lycée professor, Simone made her point by joining both the union of primary school teachers, which belonged to the CGT, and the union of secondary school teachers, which was affiliated with the more radical CGTU but had maintained its independence vis-à-vis the Communist Party. She equally supported the CGT's political independence and the CGTU's dedication to class struggle, faithfully attended meetings of both groups, and worked indefatigably to bring about their merger.

Beyond her union work, the political activities Simone plunged into upon arriving at Le Puy were of two principal kinds: continuing to teach in workingmen's adult education programs, as she had in Paris, and helping the families of the unemployed, whose ranks were particularly large in this area of south central France. The closest urban center for both of these activities was Saint-Étienne, a large mining town three hours by train from Le Puy. She traveled there the very week she arrived to meet an official of the local CGT, Urbain Thévenon, a schoolteacher who had started evening classes for blue-collar workers and had been recommended to her by Paris friends. The first impression she made on Thévenon's wife, also a schoolteacher, must have been disconcerting. "Is Thévenon here?" Simone demanded as she confronted Mme Thévenon, who stood in the doorway of her apartment, holding her darning in one hand. Upon receiving an affirmative reply, Simone brushed by her with a rude thrust of her shoulder and strode straight into the room where Thévenon was working. It seems that hostile union leaders' wives had often tried to keep her from seeing their husbands, and she had devised this way of circumventing them.

Notwithstanding this harsh initial encounter, Simone swiftly captured Albertine and Urbain Thévenon's affection. On that very first visit they invited her to dine and spend the night with them, and soon the three became inseparable. Twice a week throughout that year, "Comrade Weil," as she was known in trade union circles, made the trip to Saint-Étienne on her days off, rising at 4 A.M. on Saturdays and Sundays to teach Latin and French literature at the workers' classes Thévenon had set up. She passionately believed that in order to abolish what Marx called "the degrading division of labor into intellectual and manual work," workers must increase their verbal skills, particularly their control of written language. "The essence of the revolution consists of entering into the heritage of human culture, into the entire heritage of preceding generations,"[3] she would write the very year she arrived at Le Puy.

In the same months Simone started writing for several militant left-wing publications—*Le Cri du Peuple, L'Effort, L'École Emancipée,* and particularly *La Révolution Prolétarienne.* The latter had been founded by Revolutionary Syndicalists to save the working-class movement from two opposite dangers—corruption by bourgeois ideals and cooption by the Moscow-controlled Communist Party. However it was neither her writing nor her activism as a labor organizer that made her controversial in Le Puy; it was her support of the unemployed and her general forthrightness in displaying her political sympathies. The city council had made a token gesture toward the unemployed by creating jobs at a local quarry but offered pay that was far below subsistence level. And in December several dozen unemployed workers assembled at the mayor's home to demand better working conditions and higher wages; failing to get satisfaction from the mayor, that same day they burst in on a meeting of the city council. Although she did not speak publicly on these occasions, Simone, who had been attending these workers' meetings throughout the fall, was a member of their delegation—a problematic position for a French lycée teacher, who is officially a government functionary. The local press began a relentless battering of Simone, describing her as "a bespectacled intellectual lady with her legs sheathed in silk" (she never wore anything but thick wool stockings), and categorizing her as "one of those intellectuals who want to make a splash and flourish on the misery of the poor like mushrooms on humus." Such was the prejudice against women of her class mingling with proletarian men that the day after the incident she was summoned by the local inspector of schools, who asked her questions of striking naïveté based on reports handed him by police: Was it true that she had gone to a café with a group of unemployed? That she had shaken hands with them? That she was carrying a copy of *L'Humanité* on that occasion?

The following month, when Simone accompanied a few of the same men to yet another meeting with the mayor (although they never accepted her as one of their own, working-class folk regarded her as a big-hearted mascot), the local press escalated its rhetoric. The local right-wing paper *Le Mémorial* wrote that "Mme Weill [*sic*] red virgin of the Tribe of Levi, bearer of the Muscovite gospels, has indoctrinated the wretches." The national press joined in. In the Paris paper *Charivari* Simone was referred to as "[t]he Jewess Mme Weill, militant of Moscow." At the end of January the mayor of Le Puy asked the Ministry of Education for Simone's dismissal, and she was again summoned by the inspector of schools, who asked her to sign a request for a transfer.

Knowing her inclinations, the inspector even held out, as bait, an appointment to Saint-Quentin, an industrial city close to Paris, with a large community of blue-collar workers. But numerous protests immediately arose in her defense. Petitions attesting to her dedication as a teacher and to her uprightness as a citizen were signed by the coal miners' union of the region, by scores of her fellow professors, by many of her pupils' parents, by her own teachers' union, even by the League for the Rights of Man. Few of Simone's intimates were more supportive of her recent confrontations than her brother, André, who had recently clashed with authorities at the Indian university where he taught. He wrote her a warm letter of congratulations in which he addressed her as "Amazing Phenomenon" (in her reply she addressed him as "Dear Noumenon").

Realizing there was no hope of official censure, by February authorities in Le Puy calmed down. The city council relented, and promised to grant the stonebreakers the twenty-five-francs-a-day minimum wage they had demanded, and better working conditions.

Union agitation, writing scores of articles a year, teaching full time at the lycée, making the six-hour round trip to Saint-Étienne on weekends to hold her fastidiously prepared classes at the workmen's education center: Such hyperactivity, fueled by the constant rationale of urgent causes, is a symptom that very frequently attends eating disorders. "Simonette is killing herself with overwork," Mme Weil complained. But it wasn't to avoid overwork or controversy, both of which she thrived on, that Simone wanted to leave Le Puy. The town was too provincial, not industrialized enough. In late spring she applied for a transfer of her own accord, which must have greatly relieved the city fathers.

In the summer of 1932, at the end of the school term, Simone made a long-awaited trip to Germany. Throughout the 1920s, left-wing militants throughout Europe had looked on Germany as the probable site of the next mass-scale revolution; and Simone in particular had expressed keen sympathy for that country ever since childhood, when she had already condemned the harsh terms of the Treaty of Versailles. But in 1932 Simone had other interests in traveling to Berlin: She wanted to analyze the power base of the fast-rising Nazi Party; she wished to understand why the German working class, which was widely known to be Europe's best educated and best organized proletariat, was so deplorably drawn to Hitler.

In the elections of April 1932, Adolf Hitler's *National-sozialistische Deutsche Arbeiterpartei* had obtained 47 percent of the national vote. And by the following July, after a rash of violent strikes, these "Nazis," as they came to be called, had doubled their number of deputies in the Reichstag and become Germany's leading party. Berlin, where Simone settled for the months of August and September, was now Europe's most dangerous city, traumatized by street unrest, food shortages, assassination attempts, and unemployment on a scale unprecedented in Europe. Dr. and Mme Weil, terrified for their daughter's safety and always inventing subtle and not so subtle ways in which to protect her, decided to spend those summer months in Hamburg, some six hours away by train from the German capital, where Simone lived with a Communist working-class family. Like all the Weils she spoke fairly fluent German, and her hosts adopted her as one of their own. The only aspect of her behavior that made them uncomfortable was that she ate far less than her share, trying to leave as much food as possible for their children. *"Ihre Tochter isst wie ein Spatz,"* "Your daughter eats like a sparrow," Simone's hostess said to Mme Weil when she came to visit Simone toward the end of her stay.

Simone visited factories, met with union leaders of many persuasions, talked to hundreds of citizens at street corners and cafés. Although she would argue fiercely with him about politics, she also struck up a guarded friendship with Trotsky's son, Leon Sedov, who had gone into exile with his father and tended to adhere strictly to his ideas (Trotsky would not break openly with the Soviet brand of Communism for another few years). In letters to her friends that summer, Simone communicated her enormous enthusiasm for the stamina and intellectual mettle of the German people. "The cultural level of German workers is unbelievable . . . in comparison, the French are asleep." While deploring the way they were falling prey to Hitler's growing popularity, she particularly admired German youth. "It's hard to imagine this magnificent German working-class youth, who are active in sports, go on camping trips, sing, read . . . reduced to a military regime."[4] And her observations on Germany, which were published in the fall of 1932 in both *La Révolution Prolétarienne* and *Libre Propos,* mark a pivotal point in the development of her political ideology. Her study of the German situation led her to realize that proletarian revolutions of the kind Marxists had predicted had become impossible in her time. One reason for this impasse was that the number of white-collar employees—a class traditionally wary of any alliance with blue-collars—had grown beyond all expectations during the capitalist expansion of the 1920s. Furthermore, the sheer number of unemployed prevented the radicalization of the employed; it intimidated them into docility, since it enabled managers to fire the more rebellious workers at will.

Simone's brooding assessment of August 1932 Germany also confirmed her suspicion that Russia's Communist Party had grown totally corrupt, as had all the Communist Parties it controlled throughout Europe. What seemed to her particularly deplorable was that, although they would soon be relentlessly persecuted by the Nazis, German Communists, by concentrating their efforts on defeating their traditional enemies, the Social Democrats, had played an important role in Hitler's ascendance. In the light of contemporary historical analysis, Weil's observations strike the reader as very astute. There is one aspect of 1930s Germany, however, that is shockingly absent from her report: She makes no mention whatever of the Nazis' already vehement anti-Semitic rhetoric.

Simone's pessimism would be confirmed in the last days of January 1933, soon after her articles on Germany were published: after the Reichstag fire, which triggered a panic throughout the country, Hitler was appointed chancellor, provoking a massive exodus of Jews, trade unionists, Communists, Socialists, and leftists of all kinds. The Soviet Union, in collusion with Hitler, closed its borders to German Communists.

Shortly after returning from Germany in the fall of 1932, Simone started teaching at a lycée in Auxerre, a picturesque town three hours southeast of Paris by train. She remained in close touch with the capital, and devoted herself to finding shelter for some of the German refugees flocking into France. A parade of exiles—many of them undoubtedly spongers and double agents—now began to flood into the home of Simone's long-suffering parents. One of them, a Socialist with a Gargantuan appetite, came to stay with his girlfriend, gave Mme Weil his socks and linen to be mended, and then expressed dissatisfaction with her sewing. Another well-known Trotskyite militant who had recently had a serious falling out with Trotsky, Kurt Landau, pursued Mme Weil into the kitchen to expound his political theories, and had to hide in a back bedroom when Trotsky's son came to call on the Weils.

Simone tried to mastermind her German protégés' comforts from Auxerre, where she was not happy. The town, she found, was far more bourgeois and conventional than Le Puy, and her students, many of them daughters of career army officers, were duller. She missed the Thévenons and all her other union friends in Saint-Étienne. Her relations with the other instructors were poor. She expressed her disaffection by behaving abominably at teachers' meetings, throughout which she sat smoking, not looking up from her radical newspapers, as if deliberately trying to offend her colleagues. At home in her tiny flat, she neglected her diet more deplorably than ever, and continued to give the excess of her teacher's pay to the unemployed. Mme Weil swooped down on her daughter every few weeks, surreptitiously bribing the owner of a nearby bistro to make sure that she occasionally got a decent meal. Simone got some rest at the Christmas break, when she went to Switzerland to visit her friend from *cagne*, Simone Pétrement. Putting on skis for the first time, she insisted on climbing uphill in the most difficult way possible and fell each time she came down the run. "What willpower!" an onlooker standing next to Pétrement kept repeating as she watched Simone's extraordinary awkwardness. "What willpower!"

In the spring of 1933, just as her articles on Germany were being published, Simone wrote another essay entitled

"Perspectives: Are We Heading Toward the Proletarian Revolution?" It expressed her most stringent criticisms of Marxism and Communism to date. She focused on the fact that modern political systems could not be categorized, as Marxism had preached, into capitalist and workers' states, but were tending to fall into totally other political typologies—into the kind of totalitarianisms that had arisen in Nazi Germany and in Soviet Russia. Her accusations against the Soviet Union, which were as strong as any that had yet been made by a member of the French Left, reflected the influence of her friend Boris Souvarine, a prominent Russian-born Revolutionary Syndicalist who had played a role in the founding of the French Communist Party but was expelled some years later for insubordination.

Souvarine, a pioneer biographer of Stalin and one of the earliest, best-informed, and most vociferous left-wing critics of the Soviet Union, would soon become Simone's most beloved friend. He doubtless played a pivotal role in turning Simone against the Russian regime, and encouraged the virulence with which she attacked it from 1933 on. In the numerous trade union meetings she attended, as well as in her writings, she compared Russian communism to Hitler's National Socialism. She asserted that the Russian regime was not, as Trotsky believed, a mere "bureaucratic deformation" of the proletarian dictatorship promised by Marx, but another form of fascism. She accused both Lenin and Trotsky of having exploited the working class as ruthlessly as the most abusive capitalist entrepreneurs, with results just as devastating for the workers. "In no country, not even in Japan, are the working masses more miserable, more oppressed, more humiliated than in Russia." She also attacked the "carefully cultivated fanaticism" with which Stalin's government had brainwashed its people, and led them to accept most forms of hardship with "a mixture of mystical devotion and unbridled bestiality." The state born out of the glorious October Revolution, in her view, had turned into "a system that would methodically destroy all initiative, all culture, all thought."

The militantly anti-Soviet views put forth in Simone's "Are We Heading Toward the Proletarian Revolution?" are widely accepted today as part and parcel of our turn-of-the-century zeitgeist. One must keep in mind how heretical they were to leftist audiences in 1933. After her essay's publication in the periodical *La Révolution Prolétarienne*, an editorial in the same magazine (it was entitled "Not So Much Pessimism!") criticized Simone's "lofty intellectual resignation" and wondered what common ground it had with the Revolutionary Syndicalism she had espoused so far. Trotsky, who would not openly break with Moscow until the following year, criticized Simone harshly for defending "personality against society," a stand he categorized as "a formula of old liberalism, modernized by cheap anarchist enthusiasm." Other colleagues on the anti-Soviet Left, however, admired her article immensely. One labor leader, Marcel Martinet, believed that nothing as politically incisive had been written since Rosa Luxemburg, and Boris Souvarine judged her to be "the only distinguished intellect that the working-class movement has produced in many years."[5]

Notwithstanding Souvarine's support, Simone had to accept the fact that she was becoming anathema, among mainstream leftists, for her anti-Communist views (the first prominent French leftist intellectual to attack the Soviet Union, André Gide, did not publicize his views until 1936). The criticism Simone encountered in 1933, when she was delegated by the teachers' union to attend a meeting of the Action Committee against War and Fascism, was exemplary. When she rose to her feet to ask Communist delegates for information about the dissident socialist Victor Serge, whose reported incarceration in a Soviet jail became one of the first causes célèbres of the anti-Communist Left, she was shouted down by Stalinists. In August she would have the same experience at her own union's annual congress. Communists attending the United Federation of Teachers' convention had brought along a Soviet delegation to bolster their forces. When Simone took the platform to criticize the Soviet government for closing its borders to all German political refugees, even to Communists, she was shouted down with cries of "Viper!" and she would have been physically attacked if her friends had not formed a circle around her. It should be noted that there was a good deal of theatricality about many of Simone's political gestures. On one occasion a group of her leftist anti-Communist friends wished to pass out some pamphlets at a political meeting without provoking a confrontation with members of the Party, who readily grew violent. Disdainful of such restrictions, Simone scattered an entire packet of the leaflets from the gallery of the assembly room. The pamphlets were immediately picked up by the Communists and never reached their destined audience. The friend who reported this episode noted that she had a strong taste for "gratuitous risk and futile sacrifice."

As the school term 1932–33 came to a close, Simone had not grown any happier about her stay at Auxerre. One of her few diversions there was to engage in occasional stints of manual labor, such as digging potatoes on a workers' allotment or helping out at the shop of a Communist plumber whom she nicknamed "Robinet," "tap." (She was determined to demonstrate Communism's flaws and shortcomings, and argued with him so relentlessly that he began to suffer from extreme insomnia.) But her headaches plagued her more than ever—she was sometimes too ill to do anything at school but sit at her desk, holding her head in her hands, listening to her students read. And her relations with the administration of the Auxerre lycée did not improve. She told her students that the *bachot* was "a mere convention," and totally disdained the usual preparations for the exam. Perhaps in emulation of Alain, she taught instead a highly unorthodox curriculum that consisted of only three texts—Descartes's *Discourse on Method,* Kant's *Prolegomena,* and Plato's *Republic.* Constantly rumpling her hair as she spoke in an unchanging monotone, she interspersed her remarks with quotations from novelists and poets, particularly Tolstoy, Balzac, and Valéry's "La Jeune Parque": *"Viens mon sang, viens rougir la pale circumstance. . . ."* After sitting in on one of her classes, an inspector from the Ministry of Education reported that hers was "a distinguished mind . . . impressive in its sincerity and conviction"; but he found her lectures to be "diffuse and even quite confused," although "abundant and rich in details." So notwithstanding the generous amount of time Simone always gave her students, at the end of the school term the headmistress of the Auxerre lycée easily disposed of her by abolishing all teaching of philosophy at her school and sending her pupils to study the subject at the local boys' lycée.

After this difficult year, even Simone was ready for a vacation. She spent August in Spain with her parents and Aimé Patri, a philosophy professor and Trotskyite activist with whom she'd struck up a friendship. Her parents had seldom seen her so relaxed and happy. She swam and sunbathed much of the day, seldom getting out of her bathing suit—she was even reprimanded by the hotel manager for coming down to the dining room in her swimming gear, and asked to put on a robe. On this vacation she had shed the thick glasses and the hideous clothes with which she habitually disfigured herself, and her friend Patri remembered having been struck by her beauty.

The Ministry of Education found Simone yet another post for the fall of 1933. Her new teaching assignment was in Roanne, a large manufacturing town sixty miles northwest of Lyons. This particular lycée offered her the best teaching environment she'd enjoyed anywhere thus far. She had only five students, all of whom adored her, and her group often met in the school garden. "Our class had a truly familial atmosphere," one of her pupils recalled. "We made our first acquaintance with great thoughts in an atmosphere of total independence."[6] Although the headmistress couldn't talk her into assigning grades, and her colleagues remembered her as a "fleeting, mysterious figure immersed in some great German book such as *Das Kapital*," she was immensely respected and liked. The appointment also delighted her because it was a three-hour train ride from Saint-Étienne, close enough to resume teaching workers' courses there and to see the Thévenons often. There were no trains that could get back to Roanne after her Saturday evening classes, however. She displayed her growing need for self-abnegation by spending those nights on a leather bench in a nearby bistro, rather than with the Thévenons, waiting for the first dawn train.

From her provincial outpost Simone continued working on behalf of German refugees, and over the Christmas vacation she talked her family into sheltering their most famous guest to date, Leon Trotsky. He had left Germany the preceding July, a few months after Hitler's takeover, and had been authorized by the government of the Radical Socialist premier Édouard Daladier to live in a suburb of Paris. But he was not allowed to hold political meetings at his house, and was looking for a Paris flat in which to hold an important conference. Looking very proper and bourgeois with his goatee and moustache shaved off and his thick mane of hair slicked back and pomaded, he arrived at the Weils' home on Christmas Eve with his wife and two armed bodyguards. His party occupied the upper floor of the Weils' flat, where the bodyguards took shifts sleeping, and where Trotsky held his important political conclave a few days after his arrival. Home for the holidays, Simone also asked for an audience with "Papa," as Trotsky was called in leftist circles. Their discussion soon turned into a violent quarrel. Simone always kept her voice modulated, even in the most bitter disputes, but that day Trotsky followed his tendency to shout at the top of his voice. Dr. and Mme Weil and Mme Trotsky were in the room next door, listening intently. "This child is holding her own with Trotsky!" the revolutionary's wife exclaimed after twenty minutes. A few paragraphs of notes taken by Simone after her conversation with "Papa" have survived and are summed up here:

Simone reproached Trotsky in particular for his conduct toward the Kronstadt sailors, a group of rebellious seamen whom he ordered mercilessly shot down in 1921. "Do you belong to the Salvation Army?" Trotsky shouted. "Weil, you are a complete reactionary," he exclaimed a few moments later. "The Russian proletariat is still at the service of the productive apparatus—this is inevitable until Russia has caught up with the capitalist countries," he also said, and, "I have nothing to reproach Stalin for, save for mistakes in the framework of his political policy." "Why do you have doubts about everything?" was one of Trotsky's parting comments to Simone. However, "Papa" remained grateful for the Weils' hospitality. His meeting seemed to have been highly successful, for upon taking leave of Mme Weil he commented: "You'll be able to say that it was in your house that the Fourth International was founded."[7] In fact, he would announce the Fourth International the following summer.

While teaching at Roanne in the fall of 1933, Simone had again found herself at the center of a political storm. The president of the French Republic, Albert Lebrun, arrived in nearby Saint-Étienne in October to dedicate a new war memorial. A demonstration was called to protest his role in France's brutal suppression of a recent uprising in Indochina. As workers assembled in the main square sang the *Internationale,* Weil was hoisted to a window ledge, from which she could address the crowds. She referred to Lebrun as "a lackey of the arms merchants, the man who would let the flower of French youth and the workers of Indochina perish."[8] A few months later, in December, she again joined demonstrators, even carrying their banner, when three thousand Saint-Étienne miners marched to protest unemployment, which remained acute in France. Afterward a banquet was held at which a miner asked Simone to dance. He held her at arm's length, very delicately, proud of dancing with a professor. He was amazed by the fact that she could not keep time with him, and didn't know the basic steps of the simplest dances.

On other occasions Simone could be very ornery about keeping men at a distance, physically and emotionally. Two incidents are particularly revealing. After a meeting at a trade unionist's home in Saint-Étienne that didn't break up until long after midnight, the activists went to sleep on couches and on the floor. Simone, who had morning classes to teach, woke at 5 A.M. and got herself ready to take the first train to Roanne. A fellow unionist who knew the train schedules well, Jean Duperray, rose to tell her that the new schedule had an adequate train an hour later. Not wanting to wake his friends by talking aloud, he stood by the door, his arm thrust out as if to stop her. But Simone flung him away, hitting him in the chin with a wide swipe of her hand, like a jujitsu stroke. Recalling this incident years later, Duperray attributed the hostile gesture to Simone's migraines: She'd once told him that when suffering from particularly ferocious headaches she occasionally had a great desire to strike someone violently on the forehead (she would later make the same confession in a letter to a friend). But it is equally likely that she had actually studied jujitsu, for Simone Pétrement remembers that she was already familiar with some very effective strokes in their days at *cagne.* One can assume that Weil would have mastered the technique because of her obsessive terror of rape—it was the only crime, in her view, that justified capital punishment.

So the "sergeant-major angel," as Simone's close friends called her, was very careful not to give any occasions for romantic advances. And if, despite her tomboy manner, a man became interested in her, she discouraged him as fast as possible. She manifested her dread of sexuality at another political gathering, when a friend of hers sang an army song he had learned in Africa, whose refrain went, "I shall always remember/Theresa, my little French girl." After a few stanzas, he substituted names, and with a nod in her direction, sang, "I shall always remember/Simone, my little French girl." Did she detect, behind the allusion, some hint of tenderness to which she must put a stop? Simone stood up abruptly, looked at all the men with a very cold stare, and brought the evening to an end.

She was anything but prudish, however, about others' sexuality. As her relationship with Boris Souvarine and his mistress, Colette Peignot, attests, she was readily drawn into her close friends' love lives as adviser and confidante, and plunged into their most desolating problems as energetically as she had steeped herself in the nitty-gritty of trade union work. Peignot, a cofounder, with Souvarine, of the anti-Communist left-wing magazine *La Critique Sociale,* was a seductive, unbalanced, and notoriously promiscuous left-wing intellectual who boasted of being "the choice product of a decaying culture." She confessed to "creating a hell in sexuality,"[9] had a particular predilection for being severely whipped by her lovers, and would die in 1938, at the age of thirty-six, at the end of a tortured liaison with the surrealist/Communist writer Georges Bataille. This volatile woman's correspondence shows that during the Sturm und Drang of her relationship with Souvarine, throughout which she was hospitalized repeatedly for breakdowns and detoxification cures, Simone often played the part of nurse and general guardian. She booked doctors' appointments (sometimes with Dr. Weil) for Peignot; rode as far as Zurich, Switzerland, to visit her in various sanatoriums; spent entire days at her side; and on several occasions when Peignot threatened suicide took her home to the Weils' apartment in the middle of the night.

The depraved relationship Peignot went on to have with Bataille heightened Simone's sense of the moral stagnation of 1930s France. And her friends' tragic love triangles were probably made all the more painful for her by the fact that she was greatly infatuated with Souvarine. He was clearly the man she came closest to being in love with. ("Only Boris understands me,"[10] entries in her journals read, and, cryptically: "Boris and I, for a year and a half—dreadful severance and partial death . . ."[11]) Simone's repugnance for any form of bodily contact may have kept her from feeling any conventional physical longing for Souvarine. But this was precisely the ambivalence that was bound to deepen her tragic view of human sexuality. The Peignot-Souvarine episode, in fact, could well have turned her into a puritan, but it did not. Adoring children of all ages, she enthusiastically approved of unwed mothers who raised their offspring alone, and at times expressed envy of them. And she was fascinated by prostitutes, for whom like her mentor, Alain, she felt deep compassion. Determined to know more about their living conditions, she even asked several of her men friends to let her accompany them to brothels. This aspiration was satisfied a few years later, when a comrade arranged such a visit. But the expedition was not successful. Simone's disguise—she had dressed in men's overalls—was unmasked, and the couple was nearly lynched.

On May 1, 1934, the traditional workingmen's festival, Simone skipped classes, and joined thousands of Roanne citizens at the annual demonstration. Her students saw her in the front line of the march, fist raised, singing the *Internationale.* But by now those gestures may have been perfunctory rituals, for that year her private thoughts were going in quite another direction. Simone's hatred for the Soviet regime had become an obsession—Stalinist Russia, at that time, had few critics more severe. She often compared Stalin's dictatorship to the Reign of Terror imposed on France after the 1789 Revolution, and attributed both Terrors to the national traumas inevitably bred by war. "The Russian Revolution has evolved rather like the French one," she wrote to one of her former students at Le Puy.

> The need to wage armed struggle against an inner and outer enemy . . . resulted in the deaths of the best leaders and forced the country to hand itself over to a bureaucratic, military and police dictatorship which has nothing socialist or communist about it but the name. . . . The corruption of the Russian regime has contaminated the other Communist parties, which are entirely controlled by Moscow. The German Communist Party bears a great responsibility for Hitler's victory. The French Party continues to make the same criminal mistakes.[12]

In Simone's view, the newspaper *L'Humanité* was guilty of "as many lies as the right wing." In her growing belief that it brought little else than new forms of oppression, she had turned against the very concept of revolution, even against the nonviolent workers' uprisings advocated by the greatly diminished Revolutionary Syndicalist movement.

These dissensions with the mainstream left had already been manifested in the fall of 1933 in a debate between Simone and Georges Bataille, who in recent months had captured Colette Peignot from Souvarine. In a review of Malraux's novel *Man's Fate,* Bataille had deplored the book's negative view of revolution; and he had elaborated on his own nihilistic view of revolution as beneficially linked to values of "catastrophe and death." Simone, in an unpublished rebuttal (it was written for Souvarine and Peignot's *La*

Critique Sociale, which ceased publication when the couple broke up), criticized both Bataille and Malraux, whose devotion to the Communist Party she deplored. "What creates the . . . unity of all the [book's] characters is the notion that man cannot become fully aware of himself without intolerable anguish," she wrote about *Man's Fate,* proceeding to make a link to Pascal.

> [He] plunges into action in order to avoid that awareness. . . . For Malraux's heroes, the revolution is exactly what religion was for Pascal—a means of escaping the nothingness of one's own existence. We must seriously ask ourselves whether revolutionary action, when it derives from such a source, has any value. If it is simply a matter of fleeing from oneself, it is much simpler to gamble, or drink, or die.[13]

This was a far cry from the fiery rhetoric of Simone's student days. But however much his convictions differed from hers, she exerted a powerful fascination on Bataille, and they must have met occasionally, for he left the following portrait of her:

> Few human beings have interested me more deeply; her undeniable ugliness was repellent, but I personally felt that she also had a true beauty . . . she seduced by a very gentle, very simple authority; this was certainly an admirable being, asexual, with a sense of doom about her. Always black, black clothes, raven's wing hair, pallid skin. She was surely very kind, and she was decidedly a Don Quixote who both pleased and terrified by her lucidity, her bold pessimism, and by an extreme courage that attracted her to the impossible.[14]

At some time in the spring of 1934, Simone decided to take a year off from the lycée system and to find work in a factory. It was a curious time for her to change vocations, for at Roanne she'd had her best teaching experience to date. As she tells it, the reason for her shift of vocation was ideological. She was increasingly obsessed by the oppression of the blue-collar class, and by the following dilemma, which she considered pivotal to contemporary society: How could twentieth-century industrial production be coordinated without tyrannizing the workers? Her theories about this issue seemed to have reached an impasse, and perhaps she hoped that hands-on, physical contact might help her to find a solution. But her decision to join the labor ranks might also be seen as a token of her growing need for self-abnegation—she knew that her manual awkwardness would make factory work extremely hard. During the summer vacation, which she spent with her parents and her brother near Le Puy, she even told Simone Pétrement, who visited the Weils for a few weeks, that she was determined to "kill herself" if she could not adapt to factory life.

Simone's deepening engagement with working-class problems did not augur a return to radicalism. In fact, during that very summer of 1934, Pétrement often teased her about her growing conservatism. This change of persuasion would be displayed in her long, remarkable essay *Oppression and Liberty,* which she wrote that year over a period of six months and self-mockingly called her "magnum opus" or her "testament." Her most important text to date, it sums up her thinking on the relationship between man and society as it had evolved in the previous three years, since her graduation from Normale. Its opening passage, a stunning critique of Marxism, focuses on Marx's misplaced confidence in the

liberating potential of productive forces, which, he had predicted, would spontaneously bring about the downfall of
capitalism and the victory of the proletariat. In Simone's
view, Marx's forecast leaves many pivotal issues unresolved:
Since "productive forces" have been developing at prodigious speed for more than a century, she asks, why has the
proletariat not yet succeeded in liberating itself? And how
has one form of oppression changed into another? How has
it come to pass that the Marxist concept of capitalist ex-
ploitation has been replaced by other forms of oppression—
by slavery to the machine, and to an increasingly powerful
managerial class that dictates the running of twentieth-century
technology? In sum, the historical revelations of the 1930s,
according to Weil, were entirely undermining Marx's notions
of the proletariat as an agent of revolutionary change: The
Russian working class had been duped by its own leaders;
and the best organized proletariat in the world—Germany's—
had already capitulated to fascism.

Oppression and Liberty also features Weil's first elaboration of the concept of power, or "force," as she prefers to call
it, which would become a dominant theme in her work. Not
unlike Hobbes, she argues that all holders of power are en-
gaged in a perpetual struggle to retain their mastery, both
over those they have subordinated and against competing
power holders. Due to this contradiction at the very heart of
force, it is impossible to attain any stable domination. In her
view force "extends beyond what it is able to control; it com-
mands over and above what it can impose; it spends in excess of its own resources . . . it is made up of the opposition
between the necessarily limited character of the material
bases of power and the necessarily unlimited character of
the race for power."[15] The basic dynamic of history, she em-

phasizes, is not economic need, as Marx would have it, but this very race for power, which enslaves the strong as well as the weak. "Human history is simply the history of the servitude which makes men—oppressors and oppressed alike—the playthings of the instruments of domination they themselves have manufactured."[16] In fact, *Oppression and Liberty* is extremely pessimistic about the modern age. According to Weil, nature's original subjugation of man has been replaced by the tyranny of societal structures. The price of material progress, she tells us repeatedly, is that we are dominated by the new managerial class, the individuals who coordinate our increasingly complex commercial and industrial enterprises (this insight would be elaborated, in the postwar era, by such sociologists as James Burnham and C. Wright Mills).

But what about the second concept in the title of Weil's essay—*Liberty*? She tackles this theme last, in an austere, frugal manner: "True liberty is not defined by a relationship between desire and its satisfaction, but by a relationship between thought and action: the absolutely free man would be one whose every action proceeds from a preliminary judgment concerning the end which he set himself and the sequence of means suitable for attaining this end."[17] Any such definition of the good society must always be linked to Weil's perennial concern—the nature of work. As in Chaplin's *Modern Times,* which she saw numerous times, the central metaphor for an exploitive society is a production line whose employees labor automatically, with little incentive or free thought, under the dictatorial surveillance of a foreman. A free society, on the other hand, is characterized by a handful of human beings tackling each problem communally, and then adopting, through group consensus, the method judged best by the collective. Such a community, Weil often reminds us, is a utopia, but it can provide a criterion for evaluating the functioning of our actual lives (by the very fact that they can never become "real," she believed, utopias are less "corruptible" than concrete, practical blueprints for the future). Writing in 1934, at the dawn of the two most terrifying totalitarian systems in human history, Weil ends her essay by imploring us always to rebel against "the subordination of the individual to the collectivity." All of us must escape—so goes the marvelous last sentence—"the contagion of folly and collective frenzy by reaffirming on our own account, beyond the control of the social idol, the original pact between the individual mind and the universe."[18]

Oppression and Liberty was finished in November 1934; Mme Weil typed out the final draft of her daughter's text. This essay, too, was intended to appear in Souvarine's and Peignot's periodical, which had just ceased publication. And even though her old teacher, Alain, thought Simone's text was "of the highest grandeur," for some reason Weil did not submit it to any other periodical. She may have looked on the essay as a tool of self-enlightenment: Her motive for writing it, she would say later, was that humankind would only find ways of liberating itself when it had "understood the causes of oppression as clearly as we understand the gravity which causes a stone to fall."[19] She seemed to be aware of the essay's virtues, however, for upon the fall of France in 1940 she asked a friend to fetch it in her family's apartment, commenting that it was "worth preserving," and "very pertinent to our times." It was first published in the late 1940s by Albert Camus when he worked as an editor for Gallimard. In his introduction to *Oppression and Liberty*,

Camus wrote that "western social and political thought has not produced anything more valuable since Marx."[20]

It was midway through the composition of *Oppression and Liberty* that Simone wrote to the Ministry of Education, asking for a leave of absence from teaching. Here is how she phrased her request to the ministry: "I wish to research a philosophical essay concerning the relationship of modern technology . . . to the essential aspects of our civilization— our social organization [and] our culture."[21]

In a long letter to a former pupil at Le Puy, Simone stated that her decision to work in a factory was also related to her extreme pessimism about the political scene. She foresaw the imminent danger of a war against Germany:

> If war breaks out, Socialists and Communists will send us forth to die for "the workers' fatherland." . . . Such being the situation, it is my firm decision to take no further part in *any* political or social activities . . . here's how I foresee the future: we're about to enter a period of the most centralized and most oppressive dictatorships we've yet known in history. . . . I've taken a year's leave, in order to do a little work of my own and also make a bit of contact with the famous "real life."[22]

5. The Year of Factory Work, 1934–35

SIMONE'S DECISION TO engage in factory work as a way of understanding the plight of the working class would not have seemed outlandish to the generation coming of age in the 1930s. A few years earlier George Orwell had left his comfortable home in London to be "down and out" in Paris and London. In the United States, the Catholic activist Dorothy Day, after an affluent, bohemian youth, settled down permanently in the slums of New York's Lower East Side to begin her mission to the poor. Many American activists would follow the same path again in the 1960s. In fact, one of the finest essays on Simone Weil by an American was written by Staughton Lynd, a leader of Students for a Democratic Society (SDS), who elaborates on Weil's enormous importance to that movement. "Simone Weil may be viewed . . . as one of an international group of seekers whom I will term the first New Left," he wrote in his essay "The First New Left, and the Third." "The first New Left was made up of radicals in the years 1930–1945 who broke not only from Stalinism but also from . . . Trotskyism, and not only with Trotskyism, but in part from Marxism itself. . . . Simone Weil anticipated every major theme of the second New Left of the 1950s and 1960s."[1]

She found her first blue-collar job with the help of her friend and fellow activist Souvarine. It was with a firm called Alsthom, a large and very eminent enterprise, formed by the merger of the Alsatienne and Thompson companies, which built large-scale electrical machinery. Few members of the managerial class, in that decade, could have been persuaded to hire an eccentric, stridently left-wing intellectual and labor organizer for their production line. But Alsthom's highly progressive and enlightened director, Auguste Detoeuf, a graduate of the École Polytechnique who believed in "the synthesis of intellectual and manual work, of industry and classical culture," seemed to be very interested in the challenge of hiring such a maverick as Weil. He agreed to have her enter one of his larger Paris plants, the one on the Rue Lecourbe, in the Fifteenth Arrondissement, which employed some three hundred people and manufactured electrical parts for trams and subways. To find a rhythm of life more consistent with factory work, Simone moved out of her family's apartment and rented a tiny maid's room on the same street as the factory, wishing to live exclusively on what she earned, with no help whatever from her parents. In fact, when she went home for Sunday supper throughout the following year, she even placed the estimated sum that would have bought her share of the meal on her parents' dining room table, a habit the remarkable Weils quietly tolerated, however much it pained them.

Simone began working at Alsthom on the first Tuesday of December 1934. The director, Detoeuf, had agreed that one of her coworkers should be apprised of her identity. Many of them, noticing that her hands were not those of a manual laborer, assumed that she was an impoverished student who had failed her exams and was working at Alsthom to support herself. Noting also her extreme thinness and the fact that she was the only person in their shop who did not bring any snack to work, they often offered her hunks of their bread or chocolate, which she usually refused.

What may well have been the most intimate records of Simone's factory life—her daily letters to Souvarine—were destroyed during the Nazi occupation of Paris. So one is grateful that she kept a diary for the following eight months. Her "Factory Journal," in which she wrote almost daily while working at three different plants, records in often harrowing detail the tasks she was assigned to do for pitifully modest wages, her impressions of her fellow workers, and her own states of mind. It chronicles the degrading nature of piecemeal work, in which factory hands are paid by the item produced rather than by the hour; the deductions taken from their salaries if they do not meet the assigned quota of items; the often dangerous nature of the work; the harassing factory schedules, which offer no respite beyond a fifteen-minute lunch break; the often humiliating treatment of employees by quota-obsessed foremen. As Simone relates in her journal, she proved to be less manually awkward than she had thought. A benevolent foreman she often refers to as "Jacquot" told her that she was not as clumsy as some other workers in the shop, who maimed themselves more often than she did (admittedly, a backhanded compliment). But in view of the constant pressure for rapid production, and the lack of any safety measures, it took a great effort on her part to avoid a physical disaster. In her first months of work, she wrote to her friend Albertine Thévenon:

Imagine me standing before a huge furnace that spits out huge flames and blasts of hot air which blow straight into my face. The fire emerges from five or six large holes that are at the bottom of the furnace. I stand squarely in front of it to place scores of huge copper bobbins . . . destined for tram and subway engines. I must be very careful and make sure that none of those bobbins fall into one of the fiery holes, for they would melt; and for that purpose I must never let the pain of the burning air on my face and arms (I still bear its scars) lead me to a false motion. I lower the lid of the furnace. I wait a few minutes; I lift it again and with a hook I withdraw the red-hot bobbins, drawing them out very fast to make sure that they don't melt altogether. . . . And then the entire process starts again.[2]

On one occasion Simone's exhaustion, her headache, and the pain caused by her burns were such that she could not even manage to lower the furnace lid. She would have spoiled her day's work if a colleague had not rushed up to do it for her. ("What gratitude, at moments like these!" she reflects on this act of charity.) Extremes of cold and heat in the workplace further heightened the stress. "You pass from a machine placed in front of . . . a furnace to one exposed to terrible drafts," she jotted during a particularly cold winter week in January 1935 after noting that one of her coworkers had just had a large hunk of hair torn out by her machine. The changing rooms are not heated at all; you freeze during the five minutes it takes to wash hands and get dressed. One of the women suffers from chronic bronchitis, so much so that she must apply poultices every two days."[3] Another dangerous task assigned to Simone involved a huge cross-

beam that was used to polish large tools. The foreman repeatedly ordered her to use the beam "in a manner that was
exhausting and dangerous . . . one had to crouch each time
to avoid being hit directly in the head."[4]

Such hazards were aggravated by her fear that by not fulfilling the set quota, which was determined not only by the
quantity of pieces made but by the quality of their fashion-
ing, her day's salary would be diminished. Such judgments
were often made by capricious and ill-tempered overseers.
"796 pieces until 2:25 P.M.," she recorded one day. "Finished in 4 h. ¼. Paid out 1 fr. 12; earned 8 fr. 90 (barely more
than 2 francs an hour)."[5] Another entry: "Welding casings
all day—reached 700 at 4:30, after 8¾ hours of work. . . .
Evening: too tired to eat, remain dazed on bed."[6] What with
her frequent failure to meet the assigned quotas, her determination to live exclusively on her factory salary, and her
addictive need to purchase large quantities of cigarettes and
costly books, she was bound to have very little money left for
food. Her diet grew more negligent than ever. On a day when
her week's pay had enabled her to eat a decent evening
meal, she asked herself: "Does the meal taken at Prisunic
[one of a chain of large department stores that included
cafeterias] account for my well-being this evening?"[7] Simone's dreadful diet, as well as the strenuous tasks she was
assigned at the factory, could only worsen her chronic migraines. And a day seldom went by without her journal recording a bout of terrible pain.

Yet however severe the physical ordeals of Simone's labor, their psychological impact was far worse. What appalled her most was the humiliation of constantly being at
the mercy of someone else's orders, and the emotional and
mental aberrations inevitably caused by automation.

There are two aspects to this slavery. Speed: to "get there" one must repeat movement after movement at a pace that, being faster than the process of human thought, forbids both reflection and imagination. Upon taking up your post at the machine you must kill your soul for eight hours a day, kill your thoughts, feelings, everything . . . you must suppress, purge yourself of all of your irritation, sadness, or disgust: they would lessen the pace. You must even abolish joy.

The capriciousness of many overseers was particularly painful; the foreman at the Alsthom plant addressed his workers "in a bullying martinet tone," often leading her to wish that she could strike back at him.

From the moment you clock in at opening time until you clock out upon leaving . . . you must shut up and obey. The order can be painful or dangerous, or even impossible, to execute . . . no matter; shut up and comply. . . . If you address the chief—even concerning an urgent matter . . . you always run the risk of being upbraided; and when that happens, you must again shut up. . . . [I]n such situations thought shrivels up, retreats as flesh before a scalpel. One is deprived of full consciousness.[8]

The following passage from her journal sums up the physical and emotional toll of the assembly line with particular anguish:

Force yourself. Force yourself yet once more. Vanquish at every moment that revulsion, that paralyzing disgust. Faster. You have to double the pace. How many pieces have I made, in an hour? 600. Faster. How many, after that last hour? 650. The bell. Clock out, get dressed, leave the factory, body emptied of all vital energy, mind empty of thought, heart plunged in a dumb rage, and beyond that a sense of impotence and of submission. For the only hope for tomorrow is that they will allow me to spend yet another such day.[9]

Trying to reach "norms of speed established by merciless bureaucrats," kept "in a state of perpetual and humiliating subordination,"[10] she felt she was enduring a form of slavery that bred in her "the docility of a resigned beast of burden."[11] No wonder her favorite scene in Chaplin's *Modern Times* was the one in which a worker is chained to an experimental eating machine; designed to force-feed large numbers of workers in record time, it turns him into a helpless automaton. "At last, here's someone who experienced what I felt,"[12] she wrote a friend about the film.

Simone fell ill after seven weeks at Alsthom, in mid-January. She was diagnosed with otitis, an acute form of ear infection, and had to take a month and a half of sick leave. She spent the first weeks at her parents' flat, and then went with them for two weeks to a sanatorium town in Switzerland before returning to her job. In view of her hostility toward every aspect of the work at Alsthom, one marvels that she did not fall ill more often or get fired sooner. The certificate of service she received from the plant states that she worked there through April 5. She does not describe the conditions of her leave-taking. She might have been fired, or she might have decided to extend her scope of experience by working elsewhere; it is also possible that she had an accident on the job, for on her last day at Alsthom she notes in her diary that she suffered a bad cut on her hand. She already feels very changed, traumatized by the experience at Alsthom. "It has changed my whole view of things, even my own feelings about life," she wrote Albertine Thévenon. "I shall know joy again in the future, but there is a certain lightness of heart which I may never regain again."[13]

The following week she was looking for work at various other factories—at Issy-les-Moulineux, at Malakoff, at Saint-Cloud—and during the long stints of waiting she shared memories and reflections with the unemployed workers standing in line with her. Skilled at hiding her identity, at speaking working people's slang, and at earning their trust, she enjoyed a more total camaraderie with these strangers than in any other situation she had experienced to date. "For the first time in my life, no barriers, either in any class or gender differences . . . miraculous."[14] In one particular instance this lack of "barriers" seemed almost to lead to a sexual adventure, which of course she backed away from. While standing in line, she established a "special bond" with a worker who told her that he used to work as a foreman but had ceased to do so because he was too much of a "revolutionary" and could not "oppress his fellow workers." "His error of interpretation in regard to me," she jotted down a few days after the incident, "his attitude afterward . . . Says he will come to see me . . . the following day, a knock at the door. I'm in bed, do not open. Was it he? I'll never hear from him again."[15]

In 1935 the unemployment rate still stood at 20 percent in France, and it is remarkable that she found her second factory job within a few weeks. It was in the Boulogne-Billancourt district, at a smaller plant, Carnaud, which specialized in oilcans and gas masks. But even though its machinery was less massive and its foremen less abusive, Carnaud was physically and emotionally as draining as Alsthom. "A penal institution," she described it, "a foul, very foul institution—frantic speedup, a profusion of cut fingers, constant and massive layoffs. . . . I never once saw a worker lift her eyes off her work or exchange words with her colleague,"[16] she commented about the impersonality that prevailed at the shop. On the first day she was assigned to a stamping press that produced metal pieces, and, working with all her might, managed to make four hundred items an hour. But that afternoon the foreman, "a handsome fellow with an affable manner," came to tell her that he would dismiss her if she did not double her production to eight hundred. " 'If you can make 800 in the next two hours, *I perhaps might consent* to keep you on. There are workers who do 1,200 pieces.' "[17] Enraged, Simone pushed herself to produce six hundred pieces, but toward the end of the shift the foreman told her that it was still not enough. At six o'clock, just before clocking out, she asked the factory manager whether he wished her to return the following day. He told her she could come back, as long as she tried to work faster.

At the end of that first day at Carnaud she walked to the Seine, starved for fresh air. And as she sat by its banks—depressed, exhausted, "filled with impotent rage"—she wondered whether, if condemned to this kind of life, she would be able to "cross the Seine daily without some day throwing myself in it."[18] She had been particularly struck by a fellow worker at the factory who said to her about her thirteen-year-old son: " 'If he doesn't go to school, what will he become? A martyr like the rest of us.' "

The following morning, after summoning the strength to

produce 650 pieces on the same stamping press, she was assigned another task, which involved threading thin metal
bands at top speed, with the caution that two never be strung
adjacently. But she made a mistake and linked two bands.
The machine got stuck. The foreman had to fix it, and
seemed displeased. In such humiliating situations, she reflected, "a smile, a kind word, an instant of human contact
are worth more than the more devoted friendships amid the
privileged."

Indeed, throughout her months of factory work, Simone's
only solaces were her fellow workers' occasional expressions of kindness or sympathy. She was extraordinarily receptive to such gestures. "Each time my face is distorted by
pain, the welder seated in front of me sends me a sad smile,
full of fraternal benevolence, which does me indescribable
good."[19] "In a factory . . . the least act of kindness, from a
simple smile to a small favor, enables you to triumph over
fatigue, over the obsession of salary, over all that oppresses
you."[20] "It's enough for me to bump into a furnace-tender
with a forthright smile—to hear, in the dressing-room, an
exchange of jokes more cheerful than usual . . . these small
evidences of brotherhood bring me such joy that for a while
I don't feel the fatigue."[21] "I'll never forget that man," she
comments about an unusually kind foreman who had looked
at her with concern while she was transferring enormous
iron bolts into a packing box with her bare hands. And
throughout, she remained constantly aware of the sexist
prejudices manifested toward the women workers. "Men's
disdain for women," she noted in her factory journal, "ex-
changes of obscene jokes far more pronounced among factory workers than among others."[22] "I was in a situation

doubly inferior," she reflected later. "My dignity was not only diminished by the foremen, but also by the workers, due to the single fact that I'm a woman."[23]

She lasted at Carnaud only a month before being laid off. So far, in both plants, she had found that the emotional toll of assembly-line work was even greater than the physical stress. The single most frustrating aspect of such labor, she found, was "the total ignorance of the purpose of one's work." There was no way of relating the production of sub-machine pieces to the larger machine of which they would become a part. And there was the continuing humiliation caused by the whims of often capricious managers, a humiliation that had a profound effect on her. She would write later about that year in her life:

> I was almost broken . . . my courage, my sense of self-esteem were gradually shattered during this period . . . I rose in the morning with anguish, I went to the factory with fear; I worked like a slave; the noon pause was a painful laceration; going home at 5:45, instantly preoccupied by getting enough sleep . . . The fear—the dread— of what would follow ceased only on Saturday afternoon and Sunday morning. And the object of dread was this business of orders. The sense of personal dignity as heretofore fostered by society was broken.[24]

Fear was, indeed, her most overwhelming emotion, and she was good at putting herself in her coworkers' place, imagining how grueling it would be to be condemned to factory work for all of her life, as they were:

> Fear. Rare are those moments of the day when you're not oppressed by some anguish or other. . . . If you're not

ahead of time, the dread of the clock. At work, for those who have trouble attaining speed, the dread of not doing it fast enough. The dread of ruining pieces by forcing the rate of work, for speed produces a kind of inebriation that diminishes attention. The fear of all those accidents that can cause messed-up pieces or a broken tool. The dread, always, of a scolding. One would expose oneself to a good bit of suffering to avoid a scolding. The smallest reprimand is a great humiliation, because one can't talk back. And how many things can bring about a reprimand!! The machine was poorly set by the setter; the tool is made of poor-quality metal; some pieces cannot be put in place: here comes the scolding. . . . You must clench your teeth. Hold out. Like a swimmer treading water. But with the prospect of swimming on until the day you die. Without a boat that could ever rescue you . . .

Every gesture is the execution of an order. . . . Once at a machine, five or six movements are indicated that must be repeated at the greatest possible speed. Until when? Until you're ordered to do something else. How long will this series last? Until the chief assigns another series. How much time will you last at this machine? Until the chief orders you to go to another one. You are an object subjected to the will of another being. Since it is not natural for man to become a thing, and since there is no physical constraint, such as whips or chains, you must bend yourself to this passivity. How one would love to be able to leave one's soul in the little box where one places one's clocking ticket, and take it up again upon leaving! But one can't. . . . One must continually silence it. What else? . . . The perpetual necessity of not displeasing. The need to respond to brutal words without any nuance of ill humor, and even with deference, if you're dealing with a foreman. . . . What else? But that's enough. That's enough to show that such a life, if one submits to it, is lived "against one's will under the constraint of a driving necessity."[25]

The last phrase was a citation from Aeschylus. In her later, retrospective writings about her factory experience, Simone would often emphasize that the most harmful aspect of assembly-line work was that physical and moral suffering were gradually replaced by a state of "apathy and mental brutishness." This seems to have been constantly emphasized by her coworkers; to Weil the replacement of suffering by apathy was "the worst form of degradation. . . . A working woman who is on the assembly line, and with whom I returned on the tram, told me that after a few years . . . one ceases to suffer, even though one feels gradually stultified."

This time it is clear that she was fired, though no explanation was given for her discharge. "I don't have to account to you for anything," the foreman at Carnaud brusquely answered when she inquired about the reasons for the dismissal. A few mornings later, after some days spent in "the sinister prostration" caused by her headaches, she was standing in line again, in the rain, in front of a Renault car manufacturing plant. She went on to a dozen more factories in the following week, with no work in sight for relatively unskilled workers such as she. Ever conscious that she was, in her words, "a professor gone slumming amid the working class," she again spent hours talking with the unemployed, men and women lined up with her, recording their conversations in her diary. She was particularly struck by a woman who commented that "for seventy francs a day we'd have to put up with anything, we would have croaked." It was clear that by this time Simone was financially down and out, stubbornly refusing, as she would for years, to accept a cent from her parents, and eating less than ever. "Return to St.-Denis," she noted in her journal a week after she had been laid off. "Painful to walk so far when you're not able to eat. . . . [L]ast week I decided to spend no more than 3 fr. 50 a day in all, including transportation [the equivalent of some ten contemporary dollars]. Hunger becomes a permanent condition." Throughout the brooding reflections on food that recur in her factory journals, her cultivation of unappeased hunger seems closely linked to her impulse to self-mastery. "Is [hunger] more painful or less painful"—she repeatedly asks this searing question—"than to eat *and* do this kind of work?"[26]

She was in ill health, it was the worst time of the depression, she was temporarily a member of the most oppressed group in the labor force—unskilled female workers. In desperation, Simone took an unusual step. While standing in line in front of the Renault plant, she had heard it said that the person in charge of hiring new workers was partial to women, and tended to hire the pretty ones. And upon her next meeting with Simone Pétrement, she asked her help in putting on some makeup. For once in her life, she wanted to be pretty! Pétrement applied lipstick to Simone's mouth, and dabbed a bit of rouge on her face. "She was transformed," she recalls, commenting that it was evident she could have been a beauty "if she had taken the slightest trouble to fix herself up."[27] Pétrement accompanied Simone to the Renault plant, and reports that she was instantly hired.

At Renault, Simone was on the shift that worked from two-thirty in the afternoon until ten at night. This time she was not assigned to the stamping presses but to the even more dangerous milling machine. Notwithstanding the fact that she cut herself badly in the following weeks—in one case cuts caused by metal shavings became infected—she seemed to have done better on the milling machine than she had on the press. For she survived the one-month trial period and was rehired. So she could finally boast of a few distinct victories, such as her ability to change the cutter of the milling machine on her own (she was particularly proud of being able to place it perfectly, dead in the center of the machine). Moreover, the foreman of the Renault shop was the kindest one yet. Although she remained obsessed by "the absence of thought that plagues the slaves of modern machinery," she occasionally enjoyed the "athletic aspect" of the tough physical work. Moments of gaiety alternated with her habitual bouts of despair. "Fell asleep in the metro. A distinct act of will for each step," she noted one day. But the following morning: "A joyous day . . . less of a sense of slavery . . . tired, but all in all happy."[28]

However, by August, when the shop grew intolerably hot and stifling, her journal recorded growing exasperation. "A painful morning—My legs hurt so—I'm fed up, fed up. Those 4-by-8-centimeter pieces exasperate me, with their perpetual danger of breaking the drill hole, the need to preserve a total vacuity of mind . . . 3 false alarms, and at 11 A.M. . . . catastrophe, a broken saw tooth . . . at noon a bolt loosens the drill hole."[29] Her mood swings were severe. She suffered increasingly from the sense of "slavery" she had imposed on herself, and from the growing sense of unworthiness that had plagued her since adolescence. One morning, while getting on the bus, she asked herself: "How is it that I, a slave, can get on this bus and ride in it for my twelve *sous* just like anyone else? What an extraordinary favor! If someone brutally ordered me to get off, telling me that such comfortable forms of transportation are not for me, that I have to go on foot, I think that would seem completely natural to me."[30]

"Violent headaches, state of distress," she also wrote that summer, "the afternoon better, but weep at home of B [Boris Souvarine]."[31] Souvarine, and the handful of close friends she continued to see during her months on the production line, reported that her diet was growing increasingly limited, and in her factory journal she herself often attested to her hunger—like most anorexics, she thought obsessively about food. "Eat a bun in the morning, another at noon, three more little ones at night,"[32] she wrote in her third month at Renault. "I learn that we're getting paid today rather than tomorrow," she noted on another day, "this fills me with joy, for it means that I won't have to go without food, at noon I won't have to refuse myself anything (cigarettes, stewed fruit)."[33]

And then, toward the end of August 1935, she seems to have been dismissed from Renault. Once again her journal does not record the conditions under which she left. It is possible that she left of her own accord, since she had written to the Ministry of Education the previous May to request another teaching post. Immediately after stopping work, she drew up a balance sheet of her months on the production line. "What did I learn from this experience?" she asked herself.

Simone Weil continued to answer that question for several years. She had to address it on two levels, the personal and the historical. In terms of her own life, the most immediate impact of the factory experience was that it had detached her from "the world of intellectual abstractions" and had thrust her into a realm of "real men—good or evil, but of a genuine goodness or evil."[34] This immersion had its drawbacks: The kind of obedience she had been forced to practice all those months—a docility that repressed all reflection and functioned solely through the sordid incentives of money and fear—incited terrifying measures of self-hatred and despair. "It would be better to suffer physical abuse such as being whipped than to . . . repress all that is best in myself," she wrote a friend.

Another notable feature of Simone's personal summing up—some might call it masochistic—was her growing interest in the redemptive value of suffering. Her stints in factories reinforced her belief that suffering is the only road to spiritual growth, that it is our moral duty to endure as much physical and emotional hardship as we can bear. In that sense, factory work had brought her a "curious blend of physical pain . . . and of profound moral joy."[35] On occasion a mood of religious resignation—perhaps the first explicitly religious tone detectable in her writings—also informs her summing up of the factory experience. During those months she had often felt that she had "no right to anything, that every moment of suffering and humiliation must be received as a grace."[36] So whatever hardships it brought her, she looked on her factory year as a pivotal phase of her life, one that changed her forever. She was to describe that transformation, a few years later, to the Dominican priest Father Joseph-Marie Perrin:

> After my year in the factory . . . I was, as it were, broken in pieces, body and soul. That contact with affliction killed my youth. Until then . . . I knew quite well that

there was a great deal of affliction in the world, I was obsessed with the idea, but I had not had prolonged and firsthand experience of it. As I worked in the factory . . . the affliction of others branded my flesh and my soul. . . . What I went through there marked me in so lasting a manner that to this day when any human being, whoever he may be and in whatever circumstance, speaks to me without brutality, I can not help feeling that there must be a mistake. . . . There [at the factory] I received forever the mark of slavery. . . . Since then I have always regarded myself as a slave.[37]

"The *affliction* of others branded my flesh and my soul." The transformation she underwent during this crucial year led to a linguistic shift: The more political term of her earlier writings, "oppression," would now be replaced by the word "affliction," a notion that blends physical pain, spiritual distress, and social degradation and is pivotal to her later work.

As for the historical and political lessons Weil drew from her months on the assembly line, they were equally painful. The experience confirmed her earlier instinct that the kind of affliction suffered by factory workers produced submission rather than revolt, and made the prospect of a proletarian revolution "almost nil." While not abandoning her hopes for a fundamental restructuring of society, her previous theories of class struggle and direct action were replaced by the more pragmatic, centrist politics of the lesser evil. Her months on the production line also confirmed her belief that the aloofness of left-wing intellectuals from the ranks of trade unions greatly weakened their contributions to society, and undermined their most brilliant theorizing: "When I think that the great Bolshevik leaders proposed to create a free working class and that . . . none of them—certainly not Trotsky, and I don't think Lenin either—had ever set foot inside a factory and thus hadn't the faintest idea of the real conditions that create the workers' servitude or freedom— well—politics appears to me a sinister farce."[38]

Most of these political reflections are elaborated in a book called *La Condition Ouvrière,* a posthumous collection of Weil's writings on issues of labor and industry that Hannah Arendt immensely admired, describing it as "the only book in the huge literature on the theme of factory work which deals with the problem without prejudice and sentimentality."[39] *La Condition Ouvrière* elaborates on what Weil considers to be one of the most "demoralizing" aspects of twentieth-century industry, workers' lack of insight into the true purpose of their toil. Since they are ordered to produce the smaller fractions of true objects—the cogs and bolts of what will eventually be a motorcycle, a refrigerator, a radio—most of them create articles that they will never see in use, and look on their work as another dehumanizing routine. Such simple, humane measures as guided tours of the factory for workers' families, Weil suggests as a remedy, might enhance each individual's understanding of his or her role in the collective process. She saw some hope in the future of technology—it might diminish the repetitive aspect of much labor and leave the worker free for more thoughtful tasks.

Weil freely admitted that the proto-Marxist ideals of her earlier years had led to a distorted romantic view of factory life. And shortly after leaving Renault, in a passage possibly inspired by the futuristic machine cult of such early modernists as Filippo Marinetti and Vladimir Mayakovski, she described that naïve vision in a letter to a friend:

> A factory could become a great source of joy because of its powerful atmosphere of collective life. . . . All its noises have a meaning, all are rhythmical, they merge into a sort of great breath of shared work in which it is inebriating to take part . . . a metallic din, turning wheels, thrusts of metal; sounds that do not speak of nature or of life, but of the serious, sustained, uninterrupted impact of man on things. You merge into that great din . . . for on that sustained bass tone, continuous but ever changing, what dominates . . . is the sound of the machine that you are handling. You do not feel tiny as in a crowd, you feel indispensable. Your eyes can drink in that unity of rhythm which the entire body feels through the light vibration of all surrounding objects. In the dark hours of the morning and on winter evenings, when all is solely lit by electricity, all the senses participate in this universe in which nothing recalls nature, in which nothing is gratuitous, in which all is impact—hard, conquering impact of man upon matter. Lamps, production belts, the din, the harsh cold metal, all participate in the transformation of man into worker.[40]

"If that were the world of the factory, it would be too beautiful," she wrote a few months after that puerile utopia had been dissolved by her experience of "the famous real life." Appraising her new insights, she also noted that the Industrial Revolution had gone through two distinct stages: the most publicized phase—the transformation of production into heavy industry through the scientific utilization of inert matter—had only been the first step. The second stage, much overlooked by historians, had come after World War I and involved what she called the "scientific utilization of living matter, i.e., men." And that was why a powerful, unified trade union movement was such an urgent necessity, she wrote in summation of her factory experience: It was needed to restore the dignity of every individual; it was the only movement which was "more involved with the producer than with the production, in contrast to bourgeois society, which is interested in the production rather than in the producer."[41]

6. The Budding of Faith, 1935–38

SHE HAD ALWAYS loved the sea. "Only the sea," Simone wrote a friend in August 1935, after leaving her job at Renault, "can wash away all this accumulated fatigue." She traveled to Portugal in September with her parents, and stayed in a beautiful, stark-white little fishing village between Porto and Viana do Castelo. One day, while in the square, Simone watched a religious procession going about the ramshackle fishermen's huts that dotted the village's tiny beach. Here is how she later described this episode, the first in a series of events that were to transform her spiritual life:

> Being . . . in a wretched state physically, I entered the little Portuguese village, which, alas, was very wretched too, on the very day of the festival of its patron saint. I was alone. It was evening and there was a full moon over the sea. The fishermen's wives were making a tour of all the ships in a procession, carrying candles and singing . . . very ancient hymns of a heart-rending sadness. . . . There the conviction suddenly came to me that Christianity is pre-eminently the religion of slaves, that slaves can not help belonging to it, I among others.[1]

At the time she spoke to no one about this life-changing experience. She returned to Paris with her parents at the end of September. And a few days later (accompanied by her mother, of course), she left for her new teaching appointment in Bourges, a small provincial town with a great cathedral, three hours by car southeast of Paris. She felt more at ease there than she had in any other teaching position, and had unusually good relations with the headmistress and with her fellow teachers. The twelve students in her class, who affectionately called her "la petite Weil," enjoyed teasing her by slipping right-wing periodicals into her desk drawer. She tried to sharpen their writing skills by asking them to describe humble everyday objects in terms of one single sensation, form, or color (the winning essay in her class described an eraser). She assigned them an unusual amount of fiction and poetry, wishing them to grasp the way in which great writers express their philosophies: Homer, Racine, Rousseau, Goethe, Balzac, Stendhal, Valéry, Claudel, Saint-Exupéry, and Tolstoy's *Resurrection.* Her students were often put off by her iconoclastic views—she argued for the superiority of free unions to marriage—and by the brusque, unexpected questions she asked in order to startle them out of their conventional mindsets: "Have you ever killed anyone? . . . How many workers' houses could be built for the price of the luxury liner *Normandie*?" She greatly derided, of course, any replies that linked the ship's beauty and scale to France's prestige.

In time Simone's students came to appreciate her independence and her spartan humility. She lived in a tiny attic room she rented from a milliner. Her quarters were heated solely by a wood-burning stove and remained in a perpetual state of disorder. One day a substantial sum of money that had been lying on her desk disappeared. "Whoever took it undoubtedly needed it more than I do," she commented.

She was often seen pushing the baby carriage of a young working-class couple, and frequently visited the local hospital, where she lavished particular care on a disabled beggar. Obsessed by her experience of the previous year, unable to stop thinking about factory conditions, she approached the theme of suffering more often than ever with her students: A great many of her lecture notes that year touch on the problem of human misery. She frequently turned to Pascal for inspiration, as in the following note: "Here is what tests my valor most acutely: humiliation; degradation; slavery . . . grand idea that is at the heart of the Catholic faith (Pascal)."[2]

Simone also persevered in deepening her acquaintanceships with working-class people. With the help of the lycée's headmistress, she contacted the owner of a local plant, the Rosières Foundries, and soon after arriving went to see him in hopes of eventually getting a job at his factory. A fairly progressive man, M. Bernard had been edified by a recent visit to the United States, and published a small magazine for workers, *Entre Nous*. He asked her to contribute to his periodical, and she complied with a rousing essay, "An Appeal to the Workers at Rosières," which urged his employees publicly to share their complaints about their work. M. Bernard obviously rejected that text, but he did eventually publish a few of her short essays on Greek culture, in which she fulfilled her ideal of making literary masterpieces accessible to all. Her first essay was on Antigone; she signed these writings with the pen name "Cleanthes," after a Greek Stoic philosopher who had earned his living as a water carrier.

During her stay in Bourges, Simone also made a few attempts—most of them disastrous—to get in touch with the peasant classes. Once, when she was taking a walk in the country, she talked a farmer into letting her use his plow; to the man's fury, she quickly overturned it. Some weeks later a lycée colleague introduced her to a couple, the Bellevilles, who had a small farm in the environs. They agreed to have her come for a few hours a day and do basic tasks—dig up beetroots, prepare the cows' fodder, pile up manure, draw water for the trough. But how many questions Simone asked them as she helped them prepare the noon meal! "How much do you make? How do you make ends meet? Do you consider yourself happy?" The Bellevilles were perplexed by such queries, and never more embarrassed than when she asked them to "sum up their desires." When she asked them if she could live with them full-time, pay them rent, and "mingle with the peasants," that was the last straw. "Life would have become impossible for us," they told their daughter, pleading that Mlle Weil desist from visiting them again. Not only did she never change her clothes, they complained, but she failed to wash her hands before milking the cows, and when they offered her a fine cream cheese she pushed it away, saying that the Indochinese were hungry. "The poor young girl," they commented. "Too much study has driven her out of her wits."[3]

In contrast with her earlier years as a teacher, Simone was out of sorts during her stay at Bourges. The political situation filled her with pessimism. One would think she would have welcomed, in May 1936, the sweeping victory of Léon Blum's Popular Front, which brought in France's first Socialist premier. But although she came to respect him greatly, she was initially wary of Blum because she feared that his program of nationalization would increase the power of the state; she also mistrusted the participation of Communists in his government. As for her own state of mind, she was growing increasingly self-castigating. She felt that her worst sin was laziness. She wrote a friend about "the terrible temptation, when my courage gives out, to use my headaches as an alibi, an excuse for my idleness." She dreaded having to depend on her parents again if she stopped teaching. "One's family is a precious thing, provided it's kept at a little distance. . . . My parents' presence is a very painful burden, for with them I can't let myself go." Was she increasingly aware of the extraordinarily close— perhaps unhealthily close—ties that bound her to her mother? Might she have grown more critical of her mother's rather prehensile possessiveness? In those years she wrote a letter to Mme Weil that said: "I had a strange dream this morning . . . I dreamt that you told me 'I love you too much, I can't love anyone else,' it was horribly painful. . . ."[4]

In the spring of 1936 Simone flirted briefly with her brother's suggestion that she apply for a Rockefeller grant to study the functioning of the Tennessee Valley Authority (TVA), but she did not feel up to a trip to the United States. And she had suicidal thoughts about her headaches and continuing fatigue. "There's only one 'way out,'" she wrote a friend. "Keep on pushing myself as long as possible—and when the disproportion between the tasks to be accomplished and my ability to work will have become too great, then die . . . every time I go through a period of headaches, I ask myself whether the moment to die has not come."[5]

And then, toward the end of the school year, in June 1936, one of the most momentous political events of that decade—the general strike that followed the coming to power of Blum's Popular Front—jolted Simone out of her doldrums. A spontaneous wave of uprisings that aimed to pressure Blum into effecting sweeping social and economic reforms, it soon spread to include two million workers. And it was a brand-new kind of protest, a sit-down strike in which the workers occupied and camped in the buildings for many weeks, stringing hammocks between the machines, having food brought by friends and relatives, receiving their families, staging concerts. Simone had been scheduled to visit the Rosières plant the week the sit-ins started, but even though the commencement exercises at her school had not yet been held, she decided to pack up and go to Paris, the center of the unrest. She wrote an utterly tactless note to the director of Rosières, M. Bernard, to call off her visit, emphasizing the "feelings of unspeakable joy" the news of the strike had brought her and sending the workers her "warmest congratulations." But M. Bernard, who like almost every other factory manager in France had been aghast at the massiveness of the strikes, wrote her a scathing note that ended: "I beg you, Mademoiselle, to accept my regrets at not being able to convey you . . . anything more than my courteous regards."[6]

Back in Paris, Simone drew particular pleasure from visiting the Renault plant where she used to work. "The joy of getting into the factory with the smiling authorization of one of the workers," she wrote in an essay, "The Life and Strike of the Metal Workers," which was published in *La Révolution Prolétarienne.* "What a joy to see so many smiles there and to hear so many words of fraternal welcome. . . . What a joy to hear music, songs and laughter instead of the merciless racket of the machines. . . . What a joy to pass your bosses, standing tall. There is at last no need to struggle at every instant to conserve one's dignity."[7] By the time her article was published, the Blum government had enacted its historic legislation: a forty-hour week, the right to collective bargaining, substantial wage increases, two weeks of paid vacation a year. At the insistence of the headmistress, Simone returned to her school in Bourges for its commencement exercises. Though she had promised to wear her best clothes, she appeared in her old raincoat and her oldest, tackiest shoes. Her students clustered about her protectively, trying to shield her from public view. But, however eccentric her behavior, she enjoyed her greatest teaching success to date that year: Of her twelve students, nine were to pass their baccalaureates, a considerable achievement in any lycée. After the oral exams, Simone took a few of her graduates to see *Modern Times*—her admiration for Chaplin's insight into factory conditions remained boundless. She went so far as to say—in jest, one would hope—that along with Spinoza, he was the only great Jew.

The following fall Simone might well have been sent to a teaching post in an industrial area, as she had often requested, but history intervened. Barely two weeks after the end of her school term, the civil war broke out in Spain. In the third week of July a group of generals led by Francisco Franco staged a coup against the democratically chosen Republican, or Popular Front, government elected the previous winter. Although the success of the Spanish Popular Front had inspired the similarly named political coalition in France, French premier Blum and his sector of the moderate Left resisted the Communists' demand that France intervene in the war. Alarmed by reports that Franco was being sent supplies by Germany and manpower by Italy, Blum was wary of starting a wider European conflict. He equally feared alienating France's principal ally, Great Britain. In the wake of France's decision to stay neutral, thousands of Europeans and Americans flocked to Spain to volunteer on the Republican side.

Given our current understanding of twentieth-century history, Simone's position on France's intervention in Spain—and, more important, on pacifism in general—often seems shamefully wrongheaded. The previous March, for instance, she had wholeheartedly approved of France's decision not to intervene when Hitler invaded the Rhineland, which had been demilitarized by the Versailles treaty. Since Germany, which had only begun to rearm, could never have resisted a French army in 1936, it is now clear that France lost its chance to strike a decisive blow at Nazism. In the case of Spain, Simone's stand was a bit different: She wholeheartedly approved, again, of Blum's decision not to intervene officially against Franco. But she believed that everyone must follow his or her individual conscience concerning any war; and in the case of Spain, her conscience was dictated by her visceral sympathies for the Republicans. And so she immediately set out on the path followed later by Malraux, Saint-Exupéry, Orwell, and many other Europeans and Americans: She joined the nucleus of what would later become the International Brigades and, armed with journalist's credentials from a trade union magazine, left for the Spanish frontier to experience her first war. A few days later her parents, far more alarmed than they had been by Simone's trip to Germany, traveled to Perpignan, a town near the Spanish border, where they hoped to remain in close touch with her.

In his memoirs of the Spanish civil war, a French journalist, Charles Dreyfus, records his impression of Simone as she stood in line at the Franco-Spanish border, along with hundreds of other Republican sympathizers waiting to get through to Barcelona, clutching her press credentials:

> I can still see her, holding in her hand a small square of crumpled paper, a young woman with a Basque beret on her rather frizzy hair which hung over the spectacles perched on an aquiline nose. Her lips were finely chiseled, she wore no makeup, and her chin was forceful. Over a light grey shirt she carried a tourist bag stuffed to the brim; she wore a short dark grey skirt with knee-length socks protecting her thin legs, and was shod in climbing shoes. Her voice was soft and high-pitched and her eyes shone with intelligence. She left us quickly. The crumpled paper that she presented timidly but with a proud certainty opened up the path she wanted to follow.[8]

Once in Barcelona, Simone got her bearings by checking in at the headquarters of the Trotskyist group POUM (Partido Obrero de Unificación Marxista [Workers' Party for Marxist Unification], composed chiefly of dissidents from the Communist Party), whose leaders had heard about her during their exile in Paris the previous year. Determined to expose herself to danger, she signed up, as Orwell would a few months later, with the militia of the central anarchist trade union movement, CNT (Confederación Nacional del Trabajo [National Confederation of Labor]). The CNT militia was then fighting near a town called Pina, on the left bank of the Ebro River, the farthest point reached by the Republicans in their drive westward across Aragon. Simone quickly reached Pina and joined the column led by the legendary Buenaventura Durruti, head of the Catalan anarchist unions, who was in charge of the most important CNT militia formation, six thousand men strong. On August 15 she heard Durruti give a speech to peasants, and gravely noted his audience's lack of enthusiasm.

When she reached the front, Simone managed to get accepted into a small commando group of foreigners—French, Italians, Germans—who operated alongside the Spaniards. She was the only woman. One Carpentier, a former colonel in the French colonial army, taught her how to handle a rifle. Noting her awkwardness, her fellow volunteers immediately decided to avoid walking anywhere near her rifle's line of fire. They were also reluctant to let her join in commando missions. But she made such a scene, pleading to be included in all such operations, that she was allowed to join a group that planned to cross to the right bank of the Ebro River in order to blow up an enemy railroad line. Her party of twenty Republican supporters left by boat at 2:30 A.M. Once on the other bank, Simone was ordered to stay at base camp with the German cook as the others went on their mission. "From time to time, the young German lets out a sigh," she wrote that day in the journal that she kept intermittently throughout her stay in Spain. "He is frightened, visibly. Not me. But how intensely everything around me seems to exist!" The world, she thought, had never looked as beautiful as it did at this instant when she thought she might be killed. Yet in spite of her eagerness to see action, Simone was not that enthusiastic about the expedition. She noted the chasm between the submissive, timid local peasants and the confident, condescending, and often high-handed guerrillas in her group, and grew concerned about the violence all too often committed by her own side. "If I'm captured, I'll be executed," she wrote in her journal. "But that is what we all deserve. Our troops have shed a lot of blood. I am morally an accomplice."[9]

On the morning of August 21, as Simone's group was still bivouacked on the right bank of the Ebro, her companions started a fire in a deep pit in order to cook their meal without giving their position away. A huge pot was placed at ground level over the fire. The worst fears Simone's comrades had harbored about her physical disabilities were realized. As nearsighted as she was awkward, that night she put her foot right into the boiling oil. The burn was so bad that it extended halfway up her leg, and her skin remained stuck to her woolen sock when her friends pulled off her boots. The commandos persuaded her to take a boat to Pina, where she checked into a primitive, makeshift hospital whose head doctor was a barber. Realizing, after twenty-four hours, that her wound might be getting infected under his slipshod care, she started limping along the road back to Barcelona, laden with her knapsack, and found a ride with a Swiss trade unionist.

During the time Simone was stationed on the bank of the Ebro with her volunteer unit, Dr. and Mme Weil, cooling their heels in Perpignan, more worried than ever about their daughter's newest adventure, had pulled strings with trade unionists of their acquaintance to cross the Spanish border and get to Barcelona. Nearly all the hotels had been requisitioned. They wandered about the city with their knapsacks, searching for hours, before they could find a room. They finally found space in a dingy pension riddled with bullet holes and immediately went to POUM headquarters to search for Simone, but could get no news of her beyond the fact that she was at the front. Since the Republican troops' convoys arrived from the front at night, they stayed up past midnight several evenings in a row, sitting on a bench in front of POUM headquarters. Within four or five days Simone materialized, limping painfully but smiling, as they were sitting in a café. Dr. and Mme Weil immediately examined their daughter's leg. They feared that her infection had spread, and, failing to find any adequate medical help, Dr. Weil decided to take care of her wound himself. Simone's parents took her back to their pension, where she convalesced for three more weeks.

She used that time to take notes on the executions staged by her anarchist colleagues—a most distressing experience for her. Her fellow volunteer Carpentier came to see her at the pension, and told her the story of a fifteen-year-old boy executed by Durruti because he refused, after twenty-four hours in captivity, to take the Republican oath. She also heard of a raid staged by Republicans in which nine Fascists were killed, in revenge for nine Republicans slain in an earlier raid. Simone was obsessed and appalled by these stories. She would later describe them poignantly, along with episodes of violence she had witnessed firsthand, in a letter to the writer Georges Bernanos, whom she never met, but whose book *Les Grands Cimetières sous la Lune* she immensely admired. She was greatly moved by the way in which the notoriously right-wing Bernanos, whose sympathies lay strongly on the Franco side, deplored the brutality being perpetuated by both Nationalists and Loyalists. "One leaves as a volunteer . . . and one falls into a war which resembles those waged by mercenaries, with even more cruelty and far less regard for the enemy," she wrote Bernanos in 1938. ". . . [Y]ou're a royalist . . . who cares? I feel far more kinship for you than with my fellow militiamen i

Aragon."[10] One marvels that she conceived of a civil war in which acts of violence would *not* be committed.

Simone was still on crutches when the Weils returned to France, and would remain on them for much of the year. At the time she began her convalescence, she still had thoughts of going back to Spain. But she recuperated far too slowly. She had to request a three-month leave of absence from her teaching duties, and renewed the request twice, thus skipping the entire teaching year. But the accident had saved her life. Later that fall, a few weeks after she had left Spain, her entire volunteer unit, which had grown much larger after she left it, was cut to pieces, and every one of its women members was killed.

That autumn Simone, notwithstanding her unease at the violence they were committing in the civil war, attended meetings being held in Paris in support of the Spanish Republicans. She attacked Stalinists, as usual, and again refused to sing the *Internationale* at the end of the meeting. And although she was reluctant to admit it to anyone but her closest friends, she sensed that her sympathies for left-wing causes had been dealt another blow. She was severely disillusioned with the Spanish civil war because she felt that it had stopped representing the interests of peasants or workers and had become a strategic struggle between conflicting powers—Russia versus Italy and Germany. She tried to focus her energies again on the French trade union movement. The CGT and CGTU had recently fused into one union, as Simone had long wished they would, under the name of the older CGT, and its membership had grown to one million. She went to see the secretary-general of the organization, René Belin, about a research assignment into CGT activities in factories of northern France. He remembered that she sat modestly in a corner of his office, wearing a small beret, speaking in a fragile, delicate voice, and seemed very retiring and weak. Since her Spanish experience, much about her was softened, less abrasive, more humble. She was "chastened," many of her friends thought, and had become far less confrontational.

But she was hardly gentle or retiring when it came to attacking the Soviet Union. At a CGT meeting in February 1937, she was appalled to note that the unification of France's two major trade unions had vastly increased Communist influence. She was scandalized to see that the union's leadership had recently inserted clauses praising the USSR for "liquidating the vanguard of Fascism" through the infamous "show trials" held by Stalin in the past year (August 1936 and January 1937). She grew livid upon reading another clause in the CGT's report, which affirmed that the new Soviet constitution was "the most democratic in the world." "One can manage to tolerate a great deal of ignominy, but . . . these statements, coming on top of the bloody playacting in Moscow, somehow overflows measure," she wrote in a report on the conference for *La Révolution Prolétarienne:*

> The whole show was stage-managed along Moscow lines. . . . Impossible to describe the brutality, the baseness with which the Russian delegate expressed himself . . . concerning the last batch of Russian leaders who had been shot. . . . The claque worked efficiently. Our people . . . were paralyzed by rage or disgust. This apology for the death sentences was saluted by the Interna-

tionale sung standing up . . . some people remained
seated. . . . One takes no pride in singing the Internationale to applaud death sentences.[11]

One of the benefits of having participated in the Spanish
civil war was that it allowed Simone to support extreme
pacifist stands without being criticized for cowardice. In
January 1937 German troops landed in Spanish Morocco.
The French press called for an immediate intervention to
prevent Germany from occupying French Morocco. Arguing
militantly against intervention, Simone wrote several articles, bristling with sarcasm, to prove that France had no
rights in the first place to "Morocco, this quintessentially
French province," and had acquired it in the most repre-
hensible manner. She feigned indignation about Germany's
wish to tear Morocco away from "the traditions inherited
from its Gallic ancestors." That winter Hitler was making
signs that he might occupy the Sudetenland, and she was
equally militant about France staying out of Czechoslovakia
if the occasion for intervention arose.

In the first months of 1937, six months after returning
from Spain, Simone started attending meetings at the Café
de Flore—later made famous by the Existentialists—with a
group organized by Boris Souvarine and Auguste Detoeuf,
the enlightened director of the Alsthom factory for whom
she had worked two years previously. This coterie, which included the writers Jacques Maritain, Jean Paulhan, and De-
nis de Rougemont, among several other distinguished figures,
had just begun to publish a periodical called *Nouveaux
Cahiers*, in which Weil issued her most stunning argument
for pacifism to date. Her essay was entitled "Let Us Not
Start Another Trojan War" and was inspired by the irony-

laden pacifism of Jean Giraudoux's recent play, *La Guerre de Troie n'aura pas lieu* (in English, *Tiger at the Gates*). The play's argument is that just as the Trojan War was fought over a phantom called Helen—a person about whom the participants cared little or nothing—so contemporary wars are fought in the name of impersonal, abstract entities and "isms" such as "nation," "capitalism," "socialism." Weil issued her warning on parallel lines. At the center of any struggle for power, she wrote, lies the illusion of prestige without which power would become even less stable than it is. "Between one prestige and another there can not be any equilibrium. . . . Prestige has no bounds and its satisfaction always involves the infringement of someone else's dignity. . . . And prestige is inseparable from power . . . this seems to be an impasse from which humanity can only escape by some miracle." Anatole France, she recalled, had once deplored, in jest, that men at war believed they were dying for some industrialist. That was too rosy a picture, Simone noted with equal sarcasm: Men did not even die for anything as substantial, as tangible, as an industrialist.

In the spring of 1937 Simone fulfilled her long-held hopes to make a trip to Italy. Her migraines had grown even worse in the past months, and on her way she stopped at a clinic in Montana, Switzerland, which offered a new cure. She spent more than a month there and found little relief, but had a happy time. Dr. Weil came to visit her, and they went to Zurich to consult a celebrated ophthalmologist in hopes that he could find some clue to the mystery of her headaches. This visit was equally futile, but they took advantage of the detour to spend Easter at the nearby Abbey of Einsiedeln to listen to Gregorian chant. Dr. Weil found little interest in

Simone, who was increasingly drawn to church music, felt she could have listened to it all day long.

While staying at the sanatorium in Switzerland, Simone made a lasting friendship with a young medical student, Jean Posternak, who was undergoing a radical cure for tuberculosis (he would heal within a year and become an extremely successful doctor). It was to Posternak that most of her letters from Italy were addressed, and they give a marvelous portrait of the twenty-eight-year-old Simone—of her omnivorous cultural interests, of a craving for aesthetic beauty not often found in a nature so ascetic, and of her loyalty and tenderness to friends. One is struck by the dedication with which she instructs her ailing comrade, who has asked her to improve his knowledge of the classics. Upon arriving in Milan she copies out for him the opening stanzas of Lucretius's *De Natura Rerum,* and of Goethe's poems on Rome. She gives him a minicourse in Plato, warning him that very little of it is well translated into French. "When I'm back in Paris I'll translate some passages of the *Republic* for you, and it will serve you as a base from which to find a good text . . . or else, learn Greek, it's an easy language," she adds with the flippant attitude to scholarship typical of the gifted Weils. Simone also copies out, for Posternak's edification, two hundred lines from chapters 21 and 23 of *The Iliad,* in her own translation (she insisted on doing her own translations when she was writing about the Greeks, and often spent an hour rephrasing a single line of Homer to get it just right).

In preparation for her trip to Umbria, Simone is reading Machiavelli's *History of Florence* ("there are passages more beautiful than Tacitus, if *anything* is more beautiful than Tacitus") and copies Dante's verses on Saint Francis for her convalescing friend. As she's about to leave Milan, she describes the compositional forces in Leonardo's *Last Supper:*

> There's a point on the hair on the right side of Christ's head toward which all the perspective lines of the roof converge and also, approximately, the lines formed by the Apostles' hands on each side of him. But this convergence . . . exists only in the two-dimensional space which it evokes. Thus there is a double composition, and through a secret, subtle influence that helps to make his serenity appear supernatural, the eye is led back from everywhere toward the face of Christ. . . . There's no defensible reason not to spend one's life in the refectory of this convent.

Once in Florence, Simone spends many hours admiring her favorite painting at the Uffizi, Giorgione's *Concert.* She comments on the operas she is enjoying that month in Italy—Verdi's *Otello,* Mozart's *Nozze di Figaro* (conducted by Bruno Walter), and her favorite, Monteverdi's *Incoronazione di Poppea,* which she sees performed in the Boboli Gardens ("One of those marvels I'll remember all my life"). She also copies out for him a passage from Saint Francis's *Fioretti,* which reads, "All this, the bread we've received, the beautiful stone and this clear fountain we've discovered, are the gifts of divine Providence: that's why I want us to ask God to give his heartfelt love to this noble treasure of holy Poverty which he offers us."

While in Florence, Simone also visits the headquarters of the Fascist Party, eager to understand its mentality and its power base. She has looked up an acquaintance of Posternak, a very cordial young official of that organization, who tells her that her "normal and legitimate place in society is at the bottom of a salt mine." "I'd rather croak in a salt mine," she comments to Posternak about the young Fascist, "than to live a life as narrow-minded as this youth. A mine would be less stifling than . . . this obsession of the nation-state, this adoration of force in its most brutal state, i.e., this worship of the collectivity." This is her first mention of the "Collectivity as Great Beast" concept, a notion derived from a passage of Plato's *Republic* that elaborates on the perils of mass opinion and collective judgment. She would continue to enlarge on this "Great Beast"[12] motif, which she also used as a symbol of any excessive cult of state power, for the rest of her life.

However much she loves Rome, where she is struck by the beauty of the Pentecost Mass at Saint Peter's ("Nothing is more beautiful than the texts of the Catholic liturgy"), it's to Assisi that Simone loses her heart: "At Assisi I forgot all about Milan, Florence, Rome, and the rest." She waxes lyrical about the Umbrian landscape, "so suave, so miraculously evangelical. . . . This Saint Francis chose the most delicious sites in which to practice poverty; there was nothing of the ascetic in him." While in Assisi, she begins to ponder the fate of the human soul, which she still thinks of as mortal. "It's in this life that one must elevate oneself to eternal things," she writes her convalescing friend in Switzerland. "If all disappears with death it's far more important to not muck up the life that's given us on earth, and to save one's soul before it disappears. I'm convinced that's the real meaning of Socrates, Plato, and the Gospels, and that the rest is nothing but symbols and metaphors. The true problem of the *Phaedo* is to know if soul is a perishable substance."[13]

Although she would not describe the episode fully for another few years, it was in the Chapel of Santa Maria degli

Angeli in Assisi, where Saint Francis used to pray, that Simone had her most life-changing experience to date. "As I was alone in the little twelfth-century Romanesque chapel of Santa Maria degli Angeli, a rare wonder of purity," she wrote in 1941 to a friend, Father Perrin, "something stronger than myself compelled me, for the first time in my life, to go down on my knees."[14] So that moment in Saint Francis's chapel was the second of the pivotal experiences that brought Simone to Christianity, the first having been the religious procession in the Portuguese fishing village. Until several years later, she was extremely private about her growing commitment to Christianity.

When Simone returned to Paris, she faced more political disappointments. Léon Blum's Popular Front government, in which she had placed guarded hopes, fell, and was replaced by a coalition headed by the cautious centrist Maurice Chautemps. Writing about the demise of Blum's Popular Front in an article entitled "Meditations on a Corpse," Simone mourned his failure: "To say nothing of Blum's sincerity and morality, where shall we find his intellectual equal in French politics?" But she faulted him for not having seized imaginatively enough on the enthusiasm of June 1936, and for succumbing to the common failings of many well-meaning democratic socialists: Notwithstanding his fine intentions, he lacked that touch of pragmatic cynicism essential to efficient politics, and was hampered by his naïve proto-Marxist faith in the masses and in material progress. He would have done better, she commented, if instead of following Marx he had followed Machiavelli, who held that anyone acceding to power must take harsh measures immediately. "The fundamental principle of power and of any political activity," so she quoted Machiavelli, "is that there should never be any appearance of weakness. A force must not only make itself loved, but also, simultaneously, a little feared."[15] A few weeks after the fall of Blum, Simone suffered another great disappointment. In a turning point of the Spanish civil war, Franco captured the northwestern town of Bilbao, leaving little hope for a Republican victory. These two debacles—Blum's and the Spanish Republicans'—led her to feel more and more estranged from political activities, and may well have fueled her increasingly intense search for spiritual renewal.

Simone spent the following fall teaching at a girls' lycée in Saint-Quentin, an industrial town within easy commuting distance of Paris. Saint-Quentin was precisely the kind of working-class appointment she had desired, had been asking for, since the beginning of her teaching career. Her students must have admired her, for several of them retained the voluminous notes they took in her classes, and it is the best documented of all her teaching stints. (One of the cryptic phrases that have been preserved from Simone's lectures at the Saint-Quentin lycée: "A genius is a man who has known how to remain as intelligent at eighty as he was when he was two.") But notwithstanding the attentiveness and affection of her pupils, it was a year made wretched by her worsening headaches. They had become so intolerable that she felt her sanity was threatened. She feared madness above all else. "A time came when I thought that exhaustion and aggravated pain threatened a dreadful and total breakdown," she would write about those years. "I spent several weeks wondering whether death was not my imperative duty. . . . Only the prospect of possible death . . . brought back my serenity."[16]

Toward the end of 1937, fearing that she had a brain tumor, she visited a surgeon. When her mother objected to the possibility that she might have to undergo brain surgery, she shot back: "Do you want me to go from breakdown to breakdown?" In January 1938, as the headaches got still worse, she decided she had to ask the Ministry of Education for sick leave. She would renew the request for the rest of that school year, again for the year 1938–39, and again for the year 1939–40. In effect, she would never teach again.

This enforced idleness gave her plenty of time to study, read, and write her friends about the deteriorating political situation in Europe. Her letters to Jean Posternak, who remained in the Swiss clinic until 1938, are as eloquent a record as we have of Simone Weil's disillusionment with most of the traditional left-wing concerns to which she had dedicated herself—the working classes, the Popular Front, trade unionism. She was particularly critical of armament workers for going on strike:

> The strike of the metallurgists working for national defense is scandalous. If their actions were dictated by pacifist emotions, they would be beautiful in their affirmation of faith; but most of these workers are very far from that spirit. They're almost all in favor of armaments, particularly the Communists. Just as the government is being bled white to finance a military buildup, they're suspending fabrication to augment salaries that are already exceptionally high.

"[France] is presently a sad country," she wrote Posternak in March 1938 in the same letter, pinpointing with remarkable foresight the delusions of grandeur, the intellectual sclerosis, the moral apathy that would lead to France's defeat in 1940.

The spirit of June '36 (the Popular Front) . . . is putrefying. For anyone who'd put a measure of love and hope in the working class, the stranglehold of the Communist Party on the workers is what is most painful to watch. . . . France has just passed to the rank of a second-rate power . . . that is difficult for a people, still drunk on Louis XIV and Napoleon, which has always believed itself to be the terror and the glory of the universe. Such a transition—no one wishes to admit this—entails an incredible barrage of lies, of demagogy, of boasting admixed with panic . . . of disarray, in sum a totally intolerable atmosphere.[17]

7. Toward God and War, 1938–39

——————

IT HAD LONG BEEN an ambition of Simone's to visit Solesmes, a Benedictine abbey in northeastern France that was famous for its plainchant and was also a noted center of liturgical renewal. Its services were so popular, particularly at Eastertime, that seats were assigned months in advance, and it was difficult to get tickets to them. But in the spring of 1938 Dr. Weil, by contacting a friend in the region, was able to obtain two places for his wife and daughter. Simone and her mother spent ten days there, from Palm Sunday to Tuesday of Easter Week. Mme Weil only attended a few services, but Simone, seated at the back of the church on the left side, attended them all. "She's not a Catholic," a woman they met at the abbey commented, "yet she goes to all services more faithfully than anyone else."[1]

At no other time in her life, Simone would later write about those days at Solesmes, had she experienced such a powerful sense of Christ's Passion. She linked this epiphany of Christ's suffering to the unprecedented state of physical pain that plagued her throughout that Easter Week:

> Each sound hurt me like a blow. . . . By an extreme effort of concentration I was able to rise above this wretched flesh, to leave it to suffer by itself, heaped up in a corner,

and to find a pure and perfect joy in the unimaginable beauty of the chanting and of the words. This experience enabled me . . . to get a better understanding of the possibility of divine love in the midst of affliction . . . in the course of these services the concept of Christ's passion entered into my being once and for all.[2]

It was also at Solesmes that Simone first sensed the supernatural nature of the sacraments. This insight was inspired by a young Englishman sitting a few rows ahead of her at the abbey services; when she watched him returning from the altar after he had received communion, he seemed to emanate a "truly angelic radiance."[3] After they became acquainted she called him "angel boy." And indeed he was both angel and messenger, for he introduced her to some literature that would transfigure her life. Together they perused an anthology of seventeenth-century English metaphysical poets, in which a work by George Herbert particularly affected her. Its opening stanza reads as follows:

> Love bade me welcome; yet my soul drew back,
>   Guiltie of dust and sinne.
> But quick-ey'd love, observing me grow slack
>   From my first entrance in,
> Drew me nearer, sweetly questioning
>   If I lack'd any thing.

In view of Simone's obsessive attitude toward nourishment, one might also note that the very last lines of the poem that brought her to "divine love" have to do with food and hunger: "You must sit down, sayes Love, and taste my meat./ So I did sit and eat."

The poem's effect was very gradual. She kept rereading

it after she returned to Paris, and during the summer she seems to have learned it by heart. But it was only at the end of the year, after she'd copied it out several times for friends and recited it repeatedly, that it carried a pivotal revelation: One day, she tells us, it brought her "into Christ's presence," deepening the illumination already received at Solesmes concerning the nature of Christ's Passion. She describes a stage of that revelation, which came while she was reciting Herbert's "Love" during a particularly excruciating headache:

> At a moment of intense physical pain, while I was making the effort to love . . . I felt, while completely unprepared for it (I had never read the mystics), a presence more personal, more certain, and more real than that of a human being; it was inaccessible both to sense and to imagination, and it resembled the love that irradiates a loving being's most tender smile.[4]

Since that moment, Simone would affirm, "the name of God and the name of Christ have been more and more irresistibly mingled with my thoughts."[5]

Such experiences remain impenetrable to those who have not shared them. And in Simone's case the epiphany was particularly unexpected. Although the central mentor of her youth, Alain, had detected a mystical streak in her, she had always denied the possibility of "a real person to person contact, here on earth, between a human being and God."[6] (In light of her special kinship to Pascal, it is interesting to look back on Pascal's "night of fire," as he referred to the mystical illumination he experienced in his early thirties. In his brief description of that experience, "Memorial," a copy of which he would carry, sewn into his garments, for the rest of his life, he wrote the following: "Certitude. Certitude. Emotion. Joy. Peace. . . . Total and gentle resignation. Total submission to Jesus-Christ."[7])

The severe secularist might trace Simone's religious emergence to the myriad disenchantments she'd experienced in the social and political sphere: Passionate young woman lives through a series of traumatic disillusionments; turns away from Marxism, Revolutionary Syndicalism, trade unionism, the Spanish Republican cause; is successively shaken by her experience as a factory worker, by her disappointment at the fate of France's Popular Front, by the growing evidence of her country's moral malaise; and throughout remains very ambivalent—just as her father had been all along—about her Jewish origins.

Yet however one might try to rationalize the experience, the emotions that overtook Simone in Solesmes, and were deepened by her readings of the Herbert poem, had all the earmarks of a true mystical experience: the severe physical and emotional suffering that preceded it robbed her of all self-will; the experience came unexpectedly—she had no premonition of it; the feelings of submission, joy, and particularly of Pascalian *certitude* brought her by her epiphany (a presence "more certain and more real") were unrelated to any emotions she'd known thus far. In all these aspects of her enlightenment she follows in the tradition of a long line of spiritual authors, from Julian of Norwich and Saint Teresa of Avila to Pascal and Saint Thérèse of Lisieux. Unlike those mystics, however, and particularly unlike Pascal, who joined the Jansenist community of Port Royal shortly after his "night of fire" and never again published any text without that community's permission, Simone initially kept very silent about her spiritual awakening. In fact, she kept her religious emotions so secret that her parents had no notion of them until the fall of 1940, and her own brother would not be apprised of them until she came to the United States in 1942.

The particular surge of spiritual growth Simone experienced in 1938 was accompanied by new directions in her reading and research that were totally devoid of any political content. She began a vast program of studies in comparative religion, working her way through the Egyptian Book of the Dead and several Assyro-Babylonian texts that she was soon reading in the original ("Such a ridiculously easy language!" she exulted to Pétrement). That year she also developed a great passion for T. E. Lawrence, whom she compared to Tolstoy and Saint Francis. She had a downright adolescent crush on him: She could not bear the idea that he was dead; she was convinced that his death was a false rumor and that she might meet him in the near future. "If you wish to learn about that prodigious chemistry which makes for an authentic hero, a consummately lucid thinker, a scholar, and above all a kind of saint," she wrote Jean Posternak, "read his *The Seven Pillars of Wisdom* . . . never since the *Iliad*, as far as I know, has a war been described with such sincerity, with such a total absence of heroic rhetoric. In sum, I don't know of any historical figure, in any epoch, who so exemplifies all I admire. Military heroism is a rare thing; spiritual lucidity is even more rare; the union of the two is almost without precedent."[8]

For anyone who so took to heart the fate of Europe, the following months brought excruciating anguish. In the spring of 1938 Hitler invaded Austria, and the chances for peace grew more distant than ever. But "Peace at any price!" remained Simone's motto, as it still did for a minority of the non-Communist Left. She drafted a petition for a prominent French periodical, signed by scores of eminent left-leaning intellectuals, that appealed for immediate negotiations with "the Fascist adversary" and "salute[d] with sympathy Neville Chamberlain's efforts."[9] She feared that Hitler's *Anschluss* with Austria had increased the possibility that he would next attack the Sudetenland; she expressed those qualms in her letters to Posternak, and elaborated on them in an essay, "Europe at War over Czechoslovakia."

In Weil's view there were two scenarios in the offing for France in 1939. One was that the Czechoslovakian crisis might incite France to declare war on Germany. ("According to the Communist Party, any Franco-German war is a good war.") The other possibility was an antidemocratic coup d'état, ignited by Premier Édouard Daladier and the army, accompanied by a very violent explosion of anti-Semitism, and by brutally repressive measures against all left-wing parties. Of the two, Simone perversely thought the latter possibility—the right-wing, anti-Semitic coup—would be "less lethal" for French youth because it would not entail a full-scale war. What would be the repercussions of the Nazis' anti-Communist, anti-Semitic policies in the event that they did invade the Sudetenland? Her views on that issue, also based on the principle of the "lesser evil," were equally disturbing and shortsighted. The two million Germans in Sudetenland did have a right to self-determination, she argued, and by letting Germany occupy that area the European powers would be helping to redress an injustice that had "less chance of leading to a war." Under a German occupation, she speculated, "The Czechs can ban the Communist Party and exclude Jews from all relatively important positions without losing anything of their national life."[10]

Was it her lack of interest in her own safety, her family's ambivalence about its Jewish heritage, her masochistic streak, or a combination of all three that made Weil prefer, throughout these years, the scenarios in which she might herself be a victim? If she seemed blind to the dreadful consequences of what she considered to be a "lesser evil," it is because she suffered deeply from yet another left-wing syndrome of the 1930s—communal self-castigation about France's colonial policies. If the French wished to become worthy of freedom, so her priggish argument ran in 1938, their cause must be absolutely pure and just, and it could not become just until they let go of their colonial empire. A progressive emancipation of France's colonies, she contended with somewhat more prescience, would benefit the entire world, because it might avert wars of liberation that would bring the new nations "a frantic nationalism . . . an exacerbated militarism, and the state's invasion of all social life." (She particularly dreaded Arab nationalism.) But however genuine and deeply felt her convictions, her arguments against colonialism were sometimes pursued with a perverse left-wing logic. "To my way of feeling, there would be less shame for France even to lose part of its independence than to continue trampling the Arabs, Indochinese and others underfoot."[11] In sum, she was working under the obstinate pacifist rationale (shared, ironically, by many right-wingers and many future Vichyites) that the French nation might save itself a great deal of suffering by opening its gates to the enemy. Whereas another world war would be a disaster for the entire world, she argued, a German domination of Europe, "bitter as the prospect may be," would not be a worse prospect, in the long run, than France's colonial domination.

In retrospect Weil's position is naïve and utterly shocking, and she would berate herself agonizingly, later, for having held it.

In the summer of 1938, a few months after the *Anschluss*, Simone made her second trip to Italy, eager to see it one more time before the catastrophes she foresaw set in. This time her parents accompanied her—the Weils still loved to travel together, as they had in Simone's childhood. In Ascolo, she was threatened with a jail sentence for calling a Fascist cinema attendant a liar. At the Verona opera house, where they were attending a performance of Verdi's *Nabucco*, Simone and her mother refused to stand during the singing of Mussolini's Fascist hymn, "Giovinezza," and were finally forced to their feet when the audience baited them with shouts of "*Forestieri* [Foreigners]!" During this stay Simone made a side trip to Padua to see her favorite Giottos ("I'm soused, completely soused, from drinking in Giotto," she wrote to Posternak). She then traveled to southern France to meet with her brother, who was teaching at the University of Strasbourg, and his wife, Eveline, whom he had married the previous year. Next she went on to Switzerland to meet her parents, returning to Paris in September. She came back just before British Prime Minister Chamberlain and French Prime Minister Daladier—the later succumbing to British appeasement policies—signed the Munich Pact, which secured the cession of Czechoslovakia's Sudetenland to Germany.

Simone again signed petitions supporting Chamberlain. But even though the immediate causes of war had been avoided, she was increasingly depressed by the political situation. She spent a great deal of time, that winter, forecasting disaster. "Everything indicates that war has not been averted, but postponed," she told Pétrement. "The great expectations inherited from the three preceding centuries and above all from the last century," she wrote in an essay published that winter, "the hope of a progressive spread of knowledge, the hope of general well-being, the hope of democracy, the hope of peace—are all disintegrating rapidly."[12]

And then came the shattering moments of truth after which even Simone Weil had to abandon her pacifism. In March 1939 Hitler violated the commitments made in Munich six months earlier, and sent his troops into Prague. It took an event of this magnitude to convince Weil that in the face of Germany's aggression, pacifism was no longer an option. She finally realized that France, if enslaved, might be subjected to a military regime and would be "compelled to participate in its conqueror's wars." While fearing that there would be a terrible cost to such a victory—"the total ruin of Europe"—she faced up to the fact that the goal of the democratic powers could only be the total annihilation of Germany. Weil's mea culpa of spring 1939 did not yet acknowledge that her former pacifist stance was mistaken; she admitted only that it was no longer applicable. But in those months her writings carry the same disillusionment that had marked the most bitter passages of *Oppression and Liberty*—those in which she stated her discouragement with the workers' movement.

This series of disenchantments seemed to contribute to Simone's worsening health. In May 1939 she fell ill with pleurisy, and recovered from it so slowly that she was advised to continue her convalescence in a Swiss sanatorium. She left for Switzerland in July with two cases of books, having decided to stay away from Paris for six more months to have more time to write. Her parents, of course, decided to follow her, and met her in Geneva in August. The Geneva museum was exhibiting the treasures of the Prado, which had been evacuated at the beginning of the Spanish civil war. She visited those galleries every day, feasting for hours on her beloved Velázquezes and Goyas. Then she went on, with her family, to Nice, intending to spend the winter there. But on September 3, two days after Hitler invaded Poland, World War II was declared, and the peripatetic Weils returned to Paris. For the following few years the war would totally dictate the geography of their lives.

PART III: EXILE

Simone in New York City in 1942

8. The Debacle

THE WEILS RETURNED to a Paris filled with gaiety, to a society fraught with delusions about the might of France. There was blind faith in the invulnerability of the French Army. There was unlimited hope in the efficacy of the Maginot Line. Nightclubs thrived, and the great couturiers—Lanvin, Chanel, Piguet—continued to create spectacular collections. That season everyone danced to a British tune called "The Lambeth Walk." And one popular song began with the line, "We're going to hang our laundry on the Siegfried line," "Nous allons pendre notre linge sur la ligne Siegfried." Every citizen was outfitted with a gas mask packed into a little gray canister, and brought it along to the assigned underground shelter when sirens rang to announce an air raid test.

Throughout that fall, however, Simone remained in a state of despair. Her anguish seems to have been caused, in part, by regrets about her former pacifist delusions. But her most bitter remorse was directed at the snug safety of her daily life. She felt deeply guilty about not taking some active part in the war, not exposing herself to the same dangers as her young male compatriots. That is the frame of mind in which she conceived the notion, shortly after returning to Paris, of parachuting troops and arms into Czechoslovakia to help its people rise up against the Germans. Emphasizing that she absolutely insisted on participating—she even threatened to throw herself under a bus if the action was carried out without her—she presented her plan to several important government figures. Another utopian plan of Weil's was to organize a group of front-line nurses—small bands of specially selected women, "women of tenderness and cold resolution"—who would treat the wounded in the midst of combat. The concept was inspired by her sense that many men who die on the battlefield would survive if they were tended to earlier. Such female volunteers must be ready to sacrifice their lives, she emphasized; they would have to act with the knowledge that most of their group would be killed, and of course she was the first who wished to put her life on the line. This "front-line nurses" proposal was a particularly zany one, far better suited to World War I conditions than to those of World War II, and like most of Simone's projects it was highly idealistic—she even thought that it would actually make France's soldiers fight better, that their ardor would be heightened when "the image of the hearths they were defending appears before them as a living reality."

Beyond her anguish at the state of her country, Simone had immediate causes of concern in her own family—her brother's marriage and his status as a conscientious objector. André's union had not been accepted well by his parents. He had fallen in love with a colleague's wife, who, in 1937, had divorced her husband to marry him. Mme Weil had long hoped that her son would marry into a distinguished French Jewish family; she was initially angry at André for having chosen a divorced Gentile and refused to so much as receive her daughter-in-law, Eveline, in her home. The crisis caused by his status as a conscientious objector was yet another source of tension. Some years earlier, André had evolved a pacifist stand based on his reading of the Bhagavad Gita. At the beginning of the war he found himself in Finland, where he had been sent on a scientific mission by the French government, and bided time there with his wife, thinking it was as safe a place as any to avoid army conscription. (France, at the time, had no provisions whatever for conscientious objectors.) But Finland ceased being safe in November 1939 when it was attacked by the Russians. Absurdly suspected of being a spy—Finnish military police based their accusations on correspondence with Russian colleagues they had found in his desk—he was evicted from Finland and sent to Sweden, where he was detained for some months. In the spring of 1940 he was finally repatriated to France, where he was charged with failure to report for military duty and sentenced to five years in jail.

André's family visited him often in his jail cell in Rouen, where he and Simone enjoyed arguing about Nietzsche in ancient Greek (André worshiped the writer; Simone detested him). Simone was furious at her brother, she teased him for landing in jail before she did, and threatened to slap one of his judges in order to be imprisoned too. The Weil family's anxieties about André would not abate until well after the armistice of June 1940. In the winter of 1940, when his sentence was commuted, he wound his way to safety in Vichy France and then to South America, and arrived in the United States in 1941, a year before his parents and sister. Throughout her brother's tribulations, Simone blamed herself terribly for his decision to refuse conscription, certain that she had inspired his unbending pacifist position. The irony is that she had had nothing to do with it: Her pacifism evolved a decade after André's and was derived from totally different sources—she did not start reading the Bhagavad Gita until 1940, the second year of the war. Of the numerous religious texts she studied that year, however, it was the most influential, addressing her radical shift of views on pacifism, and her duties at a time of war.

As both Simone and André had come to understand by the beginning of World War II, the pacifist issue was far more complex than the Judeo-Christian commandment "Thou shalt not kill." The passage of the Gita that had inspired André to refuse fighting in World War II, for instance, is the one in which the warrior hero Arjuna, "filled with the deepest compassion" at the beginning of a battle that threatens to be particularly bloody, stops his chariot, wondering whether he has the heart to go on fighting. As Arjuna deliberates, the god Krishna sends him an order: "Thou must go on fighting." Krishna explains that every individual carries within him his own *dharma,* or duty, which is based on the nature of his caste; Arjuna belongs to the caste of warriors, so his particular *dharma* is to go into battle, and if he does so with total self-knowledge, he will remain pure. "The only right course is for each one of us to determine as best he can his *dharma,* which is his alone," André noted about his pacifist stand in the autobiography he published many years later. "Gauguin's *dharma* was painting. Mine . . . was to devote myself to mathematics. The sin would have been to let myself be diverted from it."[1]

It is this very same theme of the Bhagavad Gita—the concept of *dharma*—which seems to have influenced his sister, even though her reading led her to radically different conclusions. In Simone's view the collective *dharma* of France, at a moment of history when it faced the possibility of being obliterated by Nazism, was to defend itself by armed struggle; and her own individual *dharma* was to give the military cause her greatest possible support. During the following year Simone continued to meditate on many other aspects of Krishna's teaching; instead of her admiration for the Gita turning her away from Christianity, it brought her closer to it. From this time on, whenever she spoke about religion to friends (which she always did with great shyness, not wanting to reveal the depth of her spiritual commitments), she often used Krishna's name instead of the words "God" or "Christ."

To better interpret the tragedies of her time, Simone felt the need to reconsider the three main sources of Western civilization, and during the first year of the war she also pursued Greek, Roman, and Judaic studies. In an important essay she wrote during those months, "Reflections on the Origins of Hitlerism," she argued that World War II had not been caused by the innate aggressiveness of the German people, as many French citizens claimed, but by the very nature of the highly centralized modern state, which automatically breeds the impulse to dominate. She made extensive comparisons between the Nazi state and imperial Rome, "a system based entirely on force, which corrupts all that it touches," and which pursued a "politics of prestige which banishes all moral compunctions." Citing the innumerable atrocities committed by the Romans—the massacre of Carthage in 210 B.C., Caesar's own account of killing forty thousand Gauls—she contended that the leaders of both empires "enjoyed that tough, unshakeable, impenetrable, collective self-satisfaction that makes it possible to commit crimes with a perfectly untroubled conscience." Weil's "Origins of Hitlerism" has far more to say about Rome than about contemporary Germany, which is not even mentioned until midtext. And it is so vehemently critical of the authoritarian and aggressive nature of French regimes between the reigns of Louis XIV and Napoleon that when it was published in the periodical *Nouveaux Cahiers,* government censors debated half of it, on the ground that wartime conditions forbade such attacks on the motherland.

Weil's text on the origins of Hitlerism is the first full-fledged expression of her loathing for Roman culture and her adulation of Greek civilization, a preference that had been common to France's progressive, left-leaning circles since the Romantic movement (such right-wing groups as Action Française adulated Rome at the expense of Greece). And it may also be the first of her writings explicitly to berate the Jewish tradition, which she often compares to Rome's. "It was a . . . misfortune that the Jewish tradition in Christianity gave it a heritage of texts that often express a cruelty, a will to domination, an inhuman contempt for the conquered . . . and a respect for force, which are extraordinarily congenial to the Roman spirit."[2]

But the most important text by far written by Weil during the first year of the war—it remains one of her best-known and most controversial writings—is *"The Iliad,* or the Poem of Force," a memorable meditation on the workings of power in history. The only essay published in her lifetime that is not of an expressly political or social nature, it begins with the phrase, "The true hero, the real subject, the core of *The Iliad,* is might." It argues that rather than emphasizing heroism, the poem depicts human beings who are either destroyed by the intoxication of their own force or cruelly overpowered by the force of others. Blithely overlooking the

Homeric theme of martial valor as a confirmation of national and cultural identity, Weil seldom ceases to drive home her main theme: Since they "go beyond the measure of their strength . . . because they do not know its limit," all men who exercise power over others inevitably destroy themselves. Violence, in sum, is equally degrading, if not fatal, to those who impose it and to those who suffer from it. Indeed, the very bitterness, justice, and beauty of *The Iliad,* Weil notes, is this retribution—the innate impulse of the powerful to self-destruction, which is of a "geometric strictness."

"*The Iliad,* or the Poem of Force," was written at a time when Simone, unknown to her nearest and dearest, was becoming increasingly committed to Christianity. And it points to many similarities between Homer's text and the Christian Gospels. "The accounts of the Passion," she writes, "show that a divine spirit united to the flesh is altered by affliction, trembles before suffering and death, feels himself, at the moment of deepest agony, separated from men and God . . . it is this same sense which constitutes the great worth of Attic tragedy and of *The Iliad.*" She repeatedly contrasts these Greco-Christian values of heroism and compassion with the maladroit arrogance of the Hebrew and Roman traditions, which sanction cruelty because they "both believed themselves exempt from the common misery of man, the Romans by being chosen by destiny to be the rulers of the world, the Hebrews by the favor of their God."

Much has been written about Simone Weil's anti-Semitism. What has been often overlooked is that she was far more of an outsider, in her reading of the Old Testament, than anyone brought up within the Christian tradition. Reflecting her parents' agnostic views, and their indifference to most spiritual issues, she had had barely any exposure to Judeo-Christian texts of any kind. In her essay on *The Iliad,* she condemns Judaism's idolatrous, grossly materialistic view of the Godhead, "a carnal and collective deity," on two counts: It gave him the attribute of power rather than of goodness, and it impelled Jews to see themselves as God's chosen people, an exclusive, sectarian notion radically opposite to the universality of true religiousness. "Everything is of a polluted and atrocious character," she rails about the Old Testament, ". . . beginning with Abraham, right down through all his descendants (except in the case of some of the prophets: Daniel, Isaiah)."[3]

As these quotes indicate, Weil was not totally condemnatory of the Jewish tradition; she found much to redeem it from postexilic times on—not only Isaiah and Daniel but also Job, the Song of Solomon, and some of the Psalms. But she traced all the elements of Judaism she liked to foreign influences, praising the Jewish prophets, for instance, for having assimilated Chaldean ideas. Her overall judgment was brutal: "I have never been able to understand how it is possible for a reasonable mind to look on the Jehovah of the Bible and the Father who is invoked in the Gospel as one and the same being. The influence of the Old Testament and of the Roman Empire, whose tradition was continued by the Papacy, are to my mind the two essential sources of the corruption of Christianity."[4] In sum, Weil refused to accept the assertion, central to Christianity's Nicene Creed, that God had spoken through the Prophets.

It would be Weil's refusal of Judaism, quite as much as her refusal of the absolute authority of Rome, that would have made it impossible for her ever to become a bona fide member of the Catholic Church. On this crucial point, in fact, her departure from Christian doctrine was so extreme that several priests would soon label her views heretical. Reading her rantings against Judaism, one marvels: How could this brilliant a woman not realize that the most distinctive aspects of her thinking and her personality had a deep kinship with the Jewish tradition? There is her love of polemic; her penchant for Talmudically hairsplitting judgments; her tendency to rhetorical extremes; stern emphasis on an absolute obedience to God's will; the pessimistic panache with which she displayed throughout her threatened country, as Jeremiah paraded his oxens' yoke, her ashen garments and penitential self-decimation.

Weil's skewed reading of the Old Testament displays an ignorance of Judaism typical of ultrapatriotic, highly assimilated French Jews. But it was also distorted by the bizarre conception of God this spiritual freelancer had evolved over the past years, since the episode at Solesmes crystallized what one might call her para-Christian experience. Weil might well be looked on as the first postmodern theologian: scavenging from multiple sources within the ruins (or so she saw the world in 1940) of Western civilization, she assembled shards of diverse cultures into often startling juxtapositions. Just as her general philosophical views incorporated, over time, a wide variety of philosophers—Plato, Descartes, Spinoza, Pascal, Kant—so her idiosyncratic notions of the Godhead cannot be traced to any one source.

On the one hand, Weil's religious vision was deeply affected by Pascal, whose sense of a cosmic alienation, of the farawayness or absence of God, resonates throughout her work. As for her views of Creation and the origin of evil, they were very influenced by Gnosticism, which saw a radical break between the primitive, vengeful God of the Old Testa-

ment and the merciful new God of the Christians, and believed in purging Christianity of all Jewish traces. In fact,
Weil's concepts of creation, as expressed in a passage from
her posthumously published book *Waiting for God,* specifi-
cally reflect those of the second-century Gnostic heretic Mar-
cion: "On God's part creation is not an act of self-expansion
but of restraint and renunciation. God and all his creatures
are less than God alone."[5] This obviously differs severely
from the account of the universe's beginnings given in Genesis, the cradle of the Judeo-Christian tradition, which
teaches that the creation is *good,* and that all matter is a
manifestation of God's presence. In addition, Weil's view of
Creation as a falling away, as a manifestation of the *absence*
of God, reveals a Judaic facet of her thought: It is eerily akin
to the notion expressed in certain Jewish Cabalistic texts,
notably the twelfth-century *Zohar,* which saw Creation
(zimzum) as an act of retirement on God's part, a stepping
back to make room for the world. Like Weil, the Cabalists
saw Creation-as-withdrawal to be the highest possible manifestation of divine love.

Indeed, it is as if this particular Jewish scholar, when
facing the possibility of conversion, were reliving a historical drama experienced by the earliest Christians: They either had to see a continuity between the old and the new
faiths, as did Saint Paul and, nineteen centuries later, the
nun and Holocaust victim Edith Stein; or they had violently
to repudiate the religion of their fathers and turn to Gnosticism. Weil chose the second path, and her almost hysterical
repugnance for the Judaic tradition, which is all the more
ironic in the light of the Jewish influences on her work
seems to be an individual recapitulation of this great historical crisis. It may well have been dictated by a projection o

her curious self-loathing onto her people; it may have been influenced by her teacher, Alain, who was extremely critical of "this God of the Bible who is always massacring." It may also have been encouraged by her father, who had reacted strongly against the very strict Orthodoxy of his Jewish up-bringing. But these considerations hardly excuse her wrong-headedness on the issue. Many of her views on the Old Testament, such as the notion that the first chapters of Genesis were of Egyptian origin, are downright ridiculous. And her entire take on the Bible reflects her penchant for specu-lative reconstructions of history and her hazardously sub-jective manner of interpretation (when her brother, André, contested a particularly far-fetched judgment of hers, com-menting that it was "not based on anything," she replied: "It's based on what is beautiful, and if it's beautiful, it must be true").[6]

The war having interrupted the Weils' travels, they spent an increasingly anxious but uneventful winter. Only one seri-ous argument disruptive of their familial harmony is worth noting. Much pitying the young Germans whom Hitler had turned into fanatics, Simone once wondered out loud, at the dinner table, about what would happen if a young German parachutist landed on the terrace of their apartment. What would her parents do about it, she asked? Without hesita-tion the patriotic Dr. Weil answered that he would hand him over to the French police. Simone grew extremely agitated and declared that she could not sit at the table with anyone who had such intentions. The family thought at first that she was joking, but in fact she resolutely put down her fork and knife and stopped eating. She was consuming less food than ever since the beginning of the war, and in order for Simone to finish her meal Dr. Weil had to promise that he would *not* hand over the young German to the police. (This incident— one of the few reported directly by Simone's parents that touches on her eating disorders—underlines the manipula- tiveness and penchant for emotional blackmail typical of many anorexics.)

In the second week of May 1940, Germany's intensively trained troops launched their surprise blitzkrieg against the Allies, and made short shrift of Holland and Belgium. In the following ten days, Panzer divisions swept across northern France and reached the Channel, forcing the British Ex- peditionary Force to evacuate at Dunkirk. France, its mili- tary preparations weakened by the strikes that had recently plagued its war industry, much of its national resources fun- neled into the obsolete concrete of the Maginot Line, was direly unprepared. The French Army was fighting a war of the trenches based on World War I tactics. It was further dimin- ished by the utter incompetence of its high command, which was led, in André Maurois's words, by "amiable old men re- called from retirement to serve in posts considered to be ad- ministrative sinecures."[7] It continued to retreat at shocking speed. By the end of May, the torrents of refugees escaping Belgium and Flanders already impeded most Allied military maneuvers. From the windows of their apartment, the Weils began to observe tens of thousands of Parisians fleeing southward. Dr. and Mme Weil wanted to join the exodus im- mediately. But Simone, filled with her own delusions of na- tional invincibility and still hoping that Paris could defend itself against the Germans, talked them into staying.

Since Simone did not resume her journals until the last months of 1940, all we know of the Weil family's tumultuou

departure from Paris comes from Mme Weil's rather histri-
onic and possibly exaggerated accounts. They went somewhat this way:

By June 13 the Germans were within gunshot of the capital. The Weil family was out shopping that afternoon and
suddenly saw a notice declaring that Paris was an open city.
Dr. and Mme Weil finally convinced Simone that they must
leave instantly, and the three went to the Gare de Lyon just
as they were, without even returning to their apartment for
clothes. National guardsmen had surrounded the station,
forbidding anyone to enter it. Mme Weil seems to have convinced them that Dr. Weil was in charge of a medical convoy. A clerk agreed to let the doctor in, and he in turn
convinced the clerk that he could not leave without his wife
and daughter. They caught the last train to leave Paris for
the South, and the three Weils barely managed to squeeze
into the last packed car. Providentially, they carried some
money with them; Dr. Weil had had the foresight, for the
previous few days, to carry a considerable amount of cash in
his pocket whenever he left the house. The following day,
June 14, the Germans entered Paris, and from then on it
would be increasingly difficult for Jews to leave the capital.

It is clear that Simone, if left to her own fate, would have
stayed on in Paris and immediately joined some early resistance group. But in recent months she had grown realis-
tic enough about the German regime to know that her parents
would be endangered if they remained in Nazi-occupied ter-
ritory. And she agreed to get on that train with the sole purpose of getting them to safety. But she was dreadfully
anguished to leave Paris so these were not her most lucid
moments. Barely had they been on the train for half an hour

when, at a suburb of the capital, Montereau, she announced that they should get out. She was certain that the French Army was going to regain strength on the outskirts of Paris. Mme Weil countered that if a new line of defense was to be formed, it would undoubtedly be on the Loire. And she persuaded Simone to go as far as Nevers, three hours from the capital. There the Weil family encountered their friends Boris Souvarine and Auguste Detoeuf, Simone's former employer at the Alsthom plant, who arranged for the Weils to sleep in an abandoned miller's house. On June 15, their second day in Nevers, their friends warned them that the Germans would arrive soon, and offered to loan them money as needed. Simone continued to argue that Nevers would be well defended, and that the Germans' advance was about to be reversed. But Nevers was occupied that very night.

The following morning Simone and her parents stared at the Panzer divisions rolling down the main street. There were no newspapers, and German occupation forces immediately imposed a law forbidding French citizens to listen to the radio. The rumor spread that all of France was occupied. It was that very week of the Fall of France, in the miller's house in Nevers, that Simone began the habit of sleeping on the floor, a penance she would continue to impose on herself for the last three years of her life. "From now on we probably won't get the chance to sleep in any beds," she told her parents to explain why she shunned the bed provided her. But she was obviously depriving herself of this basic comfort as a gesture of solidarity with those of her nation's fighting men, and with the hundreds of thousands of refugees throughout France, who had even less of a shelter than she had. She was also manifesting that impulse to self-sacrifice she had displayed since adolescence, which would increase with terrifying intensity throughout the following years of the war.

A few days after the Germans had occupied Nevers, so Mme Weil's account of her family's exodus continues, the three Weils, in despair over the prospect that all of France might soon be under Nazi rule, started walking north along the highway to return to Paris. But just as they were leaving town, they met a former student of Simone's who was living nearby. "Do you have a radio?" Simone asked. The young woman said that she did, but feared to defy the German's ban on listening to radios. She allowed Simone to go to her house, however, and turn the radio on herself. Simone returned some minutes later, exclaiming "All of France is *not* occupied!" The Weils decided to reverse direction, and travel southward toward the Unoccupied Zone. They bought some baskets to look more like peasants (one is struck, throughout Mme Weil's tragicomic account, by the family's political naïveté) and started walking. Within a few miles, on the outskirts of a small village, a local man driving his truck pulled up to them and asked if they needed a ride south. He was a garage owner, and would do it for some money. The Weils enthusiastically agreed to meet him the next morning in a café. The village was full of Germans; the Weils did not know where to spend the night, and finally slept on the benches of the café, which was not a novelty for Simone. In the morning, with several hours' delay, the truck-driver came to pick them up and took them to Vichy.

In the beginning of the third week of June, when the Weils were still in Nevers, Premier Paul Reynaud, who favored continuing the war, if necessary from North Africa, resigned. He had rapidly lost ground to Marshal Philippe Pétain, World War I hero of Verdun. Pétain, appointed as the new premier, announced the capitulation of France on June 18. And a few days later he signed an armistice with Germany that divided France into two zones—the so-called Occupied Zone under German control, and the Free or Unoccupied Zone, also known as Vichy France. It was in the beginning of July, just as Pétain was setting up his new government there, that the Weils reached Vichy, the capital of the new Free Zone. Within a few days of arriving in Vichy, Simone met many of her Paris acquaintances. The armistice had filled her with so much rage that her mind seemed in disarray; she got into violent arguments, and displayed her anger with a theatricality that terrified many of her friends. She was passionate in her belief that the French parliament should never have agreed to an armistice, that France should have continued to fight. De Gaulle had broadcast his appeal from London on June 18, and the moment Simone heard his call to arms she resolved to join him. But obviously no one was being allowed to go to England from Vichy France: England could only be reached, with great difficulty, via Lisbon, which required a visa from Portugal, or via French North Africa, which required an "internal" visa from the Vichy government. After spending two months in Vichy, the Weils, hoping to get to Portugal within a few weeks, headed for Toulouse. There they realized that visas to Portugal or even North Africa were far more difficult to get than they had ever thought, and after two weeks in Toulouse they went on to Marseilles, where they were to spend the next eighteen months.

The hardships of *"L'Exode,"* as the French referred to the flight from the Occupied Zone, had not diminished the intensity of Simone's intellectual life. On August 6, she wrote Simone Pétrement from Vichy: "Tell me what you're doing now . . . if you are thinking of Krishna. . . . I've almost forgotten my Babylonian!"[8] In the same weeks she wrote letters to friends in Paris, asking them to go to her family's apartment—the Weils' maid had moved into it to keep it from being requisitioned by German troops—and send her some important manuscripts. Among them was *Oppression and Liberty,* which she thought "very pertinent to today." At some point during her flight from Paris—probably in Nevers—she began to write a play, *Venice Is Saved,* which she would finish shortly after arriving in Marseilles. And it was probably in Toulouse that she started taking notes for a long essay on the Cathars (also known as Albigensians), the medieval heretic sect—brutally suppressed in the thirteenth century by the kings of France and the papal Crusades—for whom she had long felt intense sympathy.

Weil saw this lost civilization of the Languedoc, which centered in Toulouse—then the third most important city of Western Europe after Rome and Venice—as the cradle of those Western humanist values currently being threatened by Nazism. The Albigensians, creators of the twelfth-century troubadour culture, had created a network of small city-states whose blend of monarchy, democracy, and decentralization Simone viewed as a model of civic virtue, and as "the only truly Christian civilization" of the Middle Ages. Their religion, although borrowing some elements from Christianity, drew its inspiration from somewhat opposite sources—neo-Platonic thought and Manichaeism. It saw the created world as evil, believed in reincarnation, and held that the body was an obstacle to spiritual perfection. (Albigensians also believed that the holiest way of death was through self-induced starvation, a detail that could not have escaped Simone.) This culture's tolerance and lack of bigotry had enabled it to live in harmony with orthodox Catholics, and in her view it understood the true meaning of force, for it "recognized that [force] was almost absolutely supreme in the world, and yet rejected it with loathing and contempt."[9] In sum, she saw the Albigensian culture as the "last living expression in Europe of pre-Roman antiquity," and it attracted her all the more because of its strong antipathy for the Old Testament.

During her stay in Marseilles, Weil would complete two essays on the Albigensians. Her discussion of *The Iliad* had been suffused with the sorrow she felt over the outbreak of World War II; in somewhat the same manner, in her essay "The Agony of a Civilization," Weil saw the Church of Rome's defeat of the Albigensians as a foreshadowing of the fate of France in 1940 (the parallel may seem eccentric and distant). The Languedoc renaissance of the twelfth century, in her view, had held far greater promise than the counterfeit official "Renaissance" that flourished three centuries later and that, particularly in France, marked the emergence of the centralized nation-state. In another of her imaginative reconstructions ("This young woman feels herself to be above history," as a Normale professor had complained), Weil saw the defeat of the Albigensian culture as the triumph of the spirit of Rome and Israel. As surely as the far greater culture of Greece had been destroyed by the Roman civilization, which brought "sterility to the Mediterranean basin," she believed that the spiritual countertradition of the Albigensians, if it had survived the onslaught of the Church of Rome, might with time have attained "a degree of creativity as high as that of Ancient Greece."

These are some of the thoughts Simone was elaborating in mid-September 1940, during her journey from Toulouse to Marseilles. When the Weils arrived in Marseilles, they still thought they could get a visa for the United States in a matter of months. It took them more than a year and a half.

9. Marseilles

A FEW WEEKS after the Weils arrived in Marseilles, legislation prohibiting the employment of Jews in government schools was issued by the Vichy government. Weil responded to the decree with a letter to the minister of education that bristled with irony and anger.

"I don't know the definition of the word Jew, this subject has never been part of my program of studies," it began:

> Does this word designate a religion? I have never entered a synagogue and I have never witnessed a Jewish religious ceremony. . . . Does this word designate a race? I have no reason to suppose that I have any sort of tie, either through my father or my mother, with the people who lived in Palestine two thousand years ago. Having pretty much learned to read by reading French writers of the seventeenth century, such as Racine and Pascal, if there is a religious tradition that I consider as my patrimony, it is the Catholic tradition. The Christian, French, Hellenic tradition is mine; the Hebrew tradition is foreign to me. . . . If nonetheless the laws demand that I regard the term "Jew," whose meaning I do not know, as an epithet applicable to my person, I am disposed to submit to it as to any other law.[1]

The letter received no reply. But in view of Weil's deep unease about her Jewishness, it calls for commentary. What is most striking is that her missive does not state her objections to a racist decree that will deprive hundreds of thousands of her fellow Jews of employment; it vents her anger, rather, at being defined by any principle of collective identity. The paradox is that this irate denial of Jewishness marks the only occasion on which she admits her parentage, if only to berate and repudiate it. In an essay on Weil that focuses on this letter, the psychoanalyst Anna Freud emphasizes Simone's self-sacrificial impulse: She argues—far too kindly—that Simone's deep estrangement from Judaism is based on the fact that she wants to remain in danger *on her own terms*.[2] But one could also see Weil's disavowal as an example of what the French scholar and concentration camp survivor Jean Améry has called "catastrophe Judaism,"[3] the experience lived by those large numbers of nonpracticing, highly assimilated Jews who were previously indifferent to their heritage and were forced to confront their Jewishness by the rise of Nazism (France was particularly rich in them). What is pitiful about Simone's particular form of "catastrophe Judaism" is that unlike Henri Bergson, Edith Stein, or Anne Frank, who reacted to this heightening of communal identity with a deepened sense of solidarity with their fellow Jews, Weil, venting her Jewish self-loathing, remains angry and alone. Most particularly unlike Bergson, whose refusal to convert was based on his fidelity to a people undergoing unprecedented persecution, Weil's refusal of baptism would be based on her sense that the Catholic Church, through its reliance on the Old Testament, was all too Jewish. In the face of the mounting threat of Nazi racism, she continues to resist any identification with the heritage that she was born into and that she finds abhorrent.

From the summer of 1940 on, Marseilles remained the gateway for thousands of refugees trying to leave France. And within a few weeks of arriving there the Weils, finally resigned to the notion that it might take many months to get a visa for the United States, settled into a spacious seventh-floor apartment on the Rue des Catalans. It was near the Old Port, and had a beautiful view over the sea. Dr. and Mme Weil carefully concealed the rental price from Simone in fear that she might refuse to live with them. And in a matter of weeks she was feeling at home in Marseilles; for just before the frontier between the Unoccupied and Occupied Zones was closed the Weils had been able to send for several trunks of belongings from their Paris flat, including their most valuable books and a number of Simone's manuscripts. She settled in to work. And she soon became an habituée at the offices of *Cahiers du Sud,* a publication, founded by playwright and filmmaker Marcel Pagnol in the 1930s, which after the fall of Paris had become the most important periodical in Vichy France, and whose cramped quarters overlooking the Old Port were the center of Marseilles intellectual life. One of *Cahiers du Sud*'s contributors, the poet Jean Tortel, described Simone Weil in those years:

> A kind of bodyless bird, withdrawn inside itself, in a large black cloak down to her ankles that she never took off, still, silent . . . alien yet attentive, both observant and distant. . . . Extremely ugly at first sight, thin, ravaged face under her large black beret, thick ragged hair, only

heavy black shoes to be seen under her ankle-length cloak—she would stare at you . . . her eyes very much to the fore as also her head and her bust, centering on whomever she watched with her invasive shortsighted-ness, with an intensity and also a kind of questioning avidity that I've never encountered elsewhere. . . . The eagerness in Weil's eyes was almost unbearable. In her presence, all "lies" were out of the question . . . her de-nuding, tearing and torn gaze . . . would grasp and render helpless the person she was looking at.[4]

The *Cahiers du Sud*, which was often in trouble with the Vichy censors because of its ultraliberal views, had a very great influence on Weil's career. Its editors' enthusiasm for her writing encouraged her to keep her journals far more faithfully than she ever had since her years of factory work. During her stay in Marseilles she filled some twenty note-books with material she wanted to incorporate into her fu-ture essays: her daily meditations, her evolving emotions about religion, those passages of literature and philosophy she particularly enjoyed. ("Misery of man without God," she quotes from Pascal during these months, and, also from his *Pensées*, "There is no harmony like the silence of God.") Her journals, which are now archived at the Bibliothèque Nationale, were also a marvel of thrift: She exclusively used the exercise books of the École Normale—bound in beige cardboard, some eleven inches wide by fourteen inches high—which its fellows received free of charge from the government, and which she seems to have stocked up on in great quantities a decade earlier.

Within a few months after she had settled in Marseilles,

Cahiers also accepted for publication the essay on *The Iliad* Weil had written the previous winter in Paris, her two texts on the Albigensians, and an essay tackling the thorny issue of French intellectuals' responsibility for the debacle of 1940. French writers, in her view, were indeed guilty of failing both literature and society by having refused to deal with the fundamental feature of the human condition, which is the opposition between good and evil: "The essential characteristic of the twentieth century is the growing weakness, and almost the disappearance, of the idea of value," she wrote.

> Dadaism and Surrealism are extreme cases; they represent the intoxication of total license. . . . Surrealists . . . have chosen the total absense of value as their supreme value. . . . Such words as spontaneity, sincerity. . . . enrichment—words that imply an almost total indifference to contrasts of value—have come more often from their pens than words that contain a reference to good and evil . . . words like virtue, nobility, honor, honesty, and generosity have become almost impossible to use or else have acquired bastard meanings.

She considered Proust to be particularly delinquent in this respect because of his undue emphasis on psychological states. "Twentieth-century literature is essentially psychological, and psychology consists in describing states of the soul . . . without any discrimination of value."[5]

Literature was never a sufficient concern for Simone, and upon arriving in Marseilles she immediately found social causes that incited her outrage. Within days she had gotten in touch with the poorest outcasts of Marseilles's underclass, the immigrant Indochinese workers drafted by the thousands at the outbreak of the war to work in ammunition factories. They were interned in a dreadful Marseilles prison, Baumettes, where thousands of men were locked up after working hours in pitch-dark unheated rooms. As a longtime critic of France's colonial policies, Simone was appalled. She wrote to the American ambassador to Vichy, Admiral William D. Leahy, to protest. She also gave most of her food coupons to the interned immigrants.

The issue of nourishment—her impulse to stop eating in sympathy with those who had less then she did—was becoming increasingly urgent for Simone. She refused ever to line up for food, and persuaded her parents never to do so either, asserting she would never eat food obtained this way. She was even more scornful about the black market. And in addition to giving most of her food coupons to the underprivileged, she further diminished her diet by sending care packages—purchased on her remaining rations—to the inmates of local internment camps in which the Vichy regime had rounded up political suspects. One of the many Paris friends she had reencountered in Marseilles, Louis Bercher, who had become a doctor, was the first to have diagnosed Simone's eating problems as a classic case of anorexia nervosa. He used the term, which had only recently come into medical literature, in the first draft (1950) of his memoir of Weil, observing that historical circumstances—the war— had reinforced her extreme sense of charity and her proclivity to self-mortification, and greatly augmented her tendency to undernourish herself. There is a certain form of intense patriotism—perhaps unique to the French, and exemplified by the poet Charles Péguy—that leads the citizen to identify corporeally with the mystical body of his or her nation.

Bercher seemed to understand that in Simone's case, she was impelled to mutilate her body in pace with the progressive decimation of France, to engrave her country's suffering into her very flesh. "She had never eaten very much, but never until the war . . . had she carried her privations as far as she did now," wrote Bercher, who linked Simone's anorexia to her general "desire for self-mortification" and her habit of sleeping on the bare floor. If only Simone had belonged to a religious order, quipped Bercher, whose own sister was a Carmelite nun, at least the Rule of Obedience would have *forced* her to eat![6]

Both Bercher and Simone Pétrement report that Weil occasionally proposed researching a scientific method of nourishing human beings solely on sunlight and certain minerals, without ever ingesting what we know as "food." Such an obsession is noted in her Marseilles journal, in which she praised the possibility of finding a chlorophyll that would permit one to feed on light. This direction of "research" alarmed both her friends. And if Bercher's remarkably lucid diagnosis of Weil's anorexia nervosa does not prevail in the early literature on her, it is because Dr. Weil, who in the postwar years insisted on verifying everything that was published about his daughter, categorically denied his younger colleague's diagnosis, and asked Bercher to strike that passage from his memoir. Bercher was able to reinstate his diagnosis of anorexia only in the version of his memoir that he published after the death of Dr. Weil, who had obviously been protecting his family from the stigmas still attached to any ailment of a neurotic nature. Neither of the doctors, of course, could have known that Simone Weil fit the profile of the average anorexic woman, as she is described in contemporary medical literature, to a tee.

Far from being the daughters, as one might think, of divorce or of dysfunctional marriages, such patients are reported to have grown up in uncommonly close, harmoniously bonded families: they tend to have no more than one sibling; their parents are usually perfectionists who place a high premium on social and intellectual achievement and have an opinion on everything; and they tend to be unusually diligent students (seeing her omnivorous foraging for knowledge, one could do an interesting study on the intellectual bulimia that accompanies Simone's anorexia). These young women typically report feeling "unworthy" and "devoid of any merit," are uncomfortable about having been born into a highly privileged life, and often reserve for the underprivileged the food they are refusing themselves.

One should also remember that as the biographies of Saint Clare of Assisi, Saint Teresa of Avila, and Saint Elizabeth of Hungary make clear, eating disorders are more the rule than the exception in the female mystical tradition. Moreover, the mother seems to be the critical parent in the creation of anorexia; one of the patient's principal motivations is to differentiate herself from the maternal body by shedding most manifestations of the reproductive process, and to generally wrest herself from maternal control. The buxom, possessive Mme Weil, with her oppressively domineering personality, her food fads, her need to control every aspect of her children's lives, might well be seen as the archetypal anorexic's mother; and such maternal character traits could only have reinforced the effects of the nutritional trauma Simone endured as an infant. Finally, contemporary research also emphasizes that there are many degrees of anorexia nervosa, ranging from severe to borderline; and these fluid diagnostic parameters would have made it increasingly difficult for Dr. Weil, if he had lived longer, to deny that Simone was suffering from some variant of the ailment.

What about Simone and the Resistance? She did, of course, immediately join whatever there was of an underground in the first months of the German occupation, and had several narrow escapes. In late 1940 Jean Tortel put her in touch with a group that had been infiltrated by several informers, and within a few weeks the Vichy police came to the Weils' flat and took her away to the police station. In case she might be imprisoned she packed a small suitcase with her copy of *The Iliad*, without which she never left the house. The arrests and interrogations took place on three different occasions. Each time Dr. and Mme Weil immediately followed their daughter and her police escort, and waited for her in a café opposite the station. The interrogations inevitably focused on accusations that she was engaging in pro-British propaganda, and on her general sympathy for England; in her correspondence with friends, which was most probably intercepted, Simone had made it clear that she looked on her forthcoming trip to the United States as a mere stepping-stone on her way to join the Free French in London; she even had a code phrase for going to England, "Doing common work with Doris." On the third interrogation the policeman, having found nothing incriminating in her answers, angrily burst out: "You little bitch, we'll have you thrown into jail with the whores!" "I've always wanted to know that milieu," Simone coolly answered. After that occasion the police ceased coming to the Weils' flat; and even though she resumed Resistance activities a few months later, when the underground groups were far more developed, that was the last time the police bothered her.

Simone found a whole new circle of friends amid Marseilles's large refugee community. With René Daumal, an acquaintance from her *cagne* days, she took lessons in Sanskrit, another language of which she had become enamored ("I hope never to stop loving these [Sanskrit] characters, which are sacred and which perhaps have never served as the vehicle of anything base").[7] Daumal introduced her to Lanza del Vasto, a prominent pacifist philosopher and follower of Gandhi whose plans to found a community on Gandhian lines filled her with enthusiasm. She spent much time with Gilbert Kahn, a literary critic and disciple of Alain who would be instrumental, later, in making her writings known. But of all the friendships she struck up in Marseilles, the most important one was with Hélène and Pierre Honnorat, the latter of whom had been a friend of André Weil's at Normale. Hélène was a devout Catholic, and it is through her that Weil met Father Perrin, the Dominican priest with whom she was to form one of her life's two or three closest bonds.

Father Perrin was a nearly blind, ascetically thin thirty-four-year-old priest whose home was the Dominican House in the east end of Marseilles. Most of the clerics in his community had very strong social commitments. Some of them anticipated the worker-priest movement of postwar France by taking jobs in factories or on the docks, and Perrin worked a great deal with refugees. He was also a great lover of Jewish culture and an accomplished Hebrew scholar, and was busy promoting Jewish-Christian dialogue in the Marseilles area. At the time Simone first tried to get in touch with him, Perrin had been preaching retreats in Africa. They finally met at the Dominican House in June 1941, and from then on Simone came to see him several times a week. "With her extreme consideration for others," Perrin recalls her visits, "she used to wait quietly in the passage, letting two or three people pass before her."

It is evident that the good priest, who was soon struck by "the extremely superficial idea she had of the Church and of Catholics," instantly saw Simone as a priceless catch: How many men in his order could boast of having converted a *Normalienne,* and a notoriously brilliant one at that? He very soon brought up the notion of baptism, but she immediately began to raise a host of objections: Baptism, she demurred, would imply an exclusive attachment to Christianity and a rejection of the truths she had found in other great religious traditions. Moreover, she was trying to get a clear answer to the issue of whether Catholic doctrine allowed for salvation outside the Church. But the most important stumbling block of all, Perrin immediately saw, was Simone's implacable hostility to Judaism. When Perrin spoke to her about his love of Jewish culture, thinking he'd find a sympathetic response, he was shocked by her belligerent antagonism. "Israel was the very citadel of all her oppositions, the nub of all her resistance [to the Church]," he reported.

Perrin became fascinated with the problem of Simone's quixotic faith, and sent her on to see another priest, Father Raymond-Leopold Bruckberger, whose memories of Simone, and of her "battling aggression," are more negative than Perrin's. "Her conversation was all dialectic, irony, attacking the front or the flank, disdaining all explanations, all rejoinders, all apologetics. . . . Were we or were we not, she demanded, the Order whose specific vocation was to reconcile the intellect with revelation?" Simone would have been a total pain in the neck, in Bruckberger's view, had it not been for two factors: She accepted such pivotal mysteries as the Trinity, the Incarnation, the Crucifixion, and the Resurrection of Christ as self-evident, in a mood of "docile reverence"; and his early impression of her arrogance was much modified when he witnessed her devotion to the Eucharist. On one occasion he came back to his chapel after a few hours of errands and found her still kneeling before the altar just as he had last seen her, contemplating the "Bread of Life" that she was refusing herself, "nailed to the spot by a prodigious attention," as he described her, "exposed, offered to the irradiation of the Invisible Presence."[8]

The Dominicans would soon have some respite from Simone's intellectual battering. The prospect of leaving France still being fairly remote, she was again obsessed with the notion of doing hard physical labor, and since meeting Father Perrin she had badgered him to find her work as a "farm servant" in the Provence countryside. He arranged such employment with friends of his, the Thibons, in Saint-Marcel d'Ardèche, one hundred miles north of Marseilles. Gustave Thibon was a self-taught Catholic philosopher of distinctly right-wing persuasion—many of Weil's biographers have overlooked the fact that he was one of Marshal Pétain's principal speechwriters—who had published a few books on mysticism and was a particular scholar of Saint John of the Cross. He agreed, after some hesitation, to take Simone into his house. She left for Saint-Marcel on August 7.

Thibon was to become the single most important chronicler of Simone's personality. His first impressions of her focus on her weakened appearance. He found her "prematurely bent and old looking due to asceticism and illness . . . her magnificent eyes alone triumphing in this shipwreck of beauty. . . . I had the impression of being face to face with an individual who was radically foreign to all my ways of thinking and feeling and . . . to all that represented the meaning and savor of existence," he recalled, "one who refused to make any concession whatever to the requirements and conventions of social life." From the moment they met, Simone started to plague Thibon with complications. She refused the bedroom that had been prepared for her in his very modest house, finding it "too comfortable," and declared that she would sleep outdoors. After some persuasion, she eventually compromised on a half-ruined little hut on the banks of the Rhône, two and a half miles from Thibon's home, that belonged to his in-laws. In one room she placed her sleeping bag on top of a mound of pine needles, in another she installed her worktable; the arrangements delighted her. Thibon notes that she did her farmwork—getting up at 5 A.M. to milk cows, putting fodder out for the cattle, helping his wife with the housework and kitchen—with "an inflexible energy," and with "a clumsiness only equaled by her good will, the latter ending by triumphing over the former."[9] She often shared meals with her hosts, eating barely enough to keep body and soul together, always pleading the stringencies of rationing as an excuse for her scant diet. In the evenings she sat outdoors with Thibon, helping him improve his Greek, reading Plato's *Phaedo* with him in the original. Thibon heaps praise on her gifts as a teacher: "She knew how to place herself on the level of any pupil whatsoever . . . and brought to the task . . . that quality of extreme attention which, in her doctrine, is closely associated with prayer." He recalled her as "a charming and lively companion" with a keen sense of humor and high spirits whose extraordinary learning gave her conversation "an unforgettable charm." Thibon and Weil had their share of arguments, particularly about the Vichy government and about German Romanticism, both of which Simone was extremely critical of. "She went on ad infinitum in an inexorably monotonous voice," Thibon reports. "I emerged from these endless discussions literally worn out."[10] But however intractable her opinions, he notes, she greatly enjoyed being contradicted and always wished to argue some more.

Simone's days with the Thibons—their blend of solitude, manual labor, and occasional intellectual companionship—were as idyllically happy as any she had ever known. "Admirable landscape, delicious air, rest, leisure, solitude, fresh fruits and vegetables . . . the only danger I run is losing myself among these sensual pleasures,"[11] she wrote her parents. Her happiness in the Ardèche even led her to suggest that the Weils should all three settle somewhere in the surrounding countryside if they failed to get to the United States. Dr. Weil could practice medicine, they would grow their own vegetables, Simone would write and give some lessons. In September Dr. and Mme Weil came to see her for a week, staying at a tiny inn in the village. Thibon found Selma too domineering and inquisitive, but took a great liking to the kind, amiable Dr. Weil and his repertory of "vaguely anti-Semitic jokes."

As for Thibon's long-term impression of Simone, by the last weeks of her stay he acquired "a sense of veneration" for her powers of religious insight, powers he had only ascribed to the greatest theologians and mystics. However, there are a few critical undertones in Thibon's sagacious summing up. He intimates that she longed for surrender but lacked the ultimate confidence to hand over her treasured contradictions into God's care (one might well argue that her need to maintain control over her every mental process might have been linked to her anorexic's impulse to retain absolute command over her body). Moreover, Thibon notes, although Simone strived for detachment, "she was not detached from her own detachment." She did not seem to realize, in fact, the grave complications she caused in the lives of others when she undertook to fulfill her extraordinarily self-centered vocation for self-effacement. "This soul who wanted to be flexible to every movement of the divine will," he wrote, "could not bear the course of events, or the kindness of her friends, altering by one iota the positioning of the stakes with which she had marked the path of self-immolation . . . the way she mounted guard around her void still displayed a terrible preoccupation with herself."[12] In view of the reams of Weilian hagiography, Thibon's sternness is bracing. There are many times one wants to shake Simone by the shoulders and say, "Come off it, you spoiled brat—get off your high horse!" At moments the pigheadedness of her search for purity is so infuriating that one is tempted to sympathize with a very severe critic, the poet Kenneth Rexroth. Rexroth wrote that she needed "the vulgar but holy frivolity" of an unsophisticated parish priest, the kind who would have told her, "'Come, my child, what you need is to get baptized, obey the ten commandments, go to Mass on Sundays . . . put some meat on your bones, and get a husband.'"[13]

However much she loved her life with the Thibons, Simone knew she could not encroach anymore on their hospitality, and anyhow she wanted to find more arduous physical labor. Thibon had found her employment in a vineyard a few miles away, at Saint-Julien de Peyrolas, for the forthcoming harvest. She had ten days to spare before the *vendange* began, and spent them with her parents in a little town in the French Alps. Simone Pétrement came for a few days, and found her much changed. She had lost none of her sense of humor, but displayed a new level of "gentleness and serenity . . . with a more tender, wiser goodness."[14] The two friends talked ceaselessly: of the Upanishads, which Simone was now reading in Sanskrit; of the drawbacks to Hegel's dialectic; of the project for front-line nurses which Simone still kept as a priority. Pétrement noted that Simone often read a copy of Saint John of the Cross that Thibon had given her, and that she seemed to pray in a new way: Along with Thibon, she had recently learned the Our Father in the original Greek, and was so astonished by its beauty that she repeated it over and over again in a manner that greatly intensified her religious vision: "The infinite sweetness of this Greek text so took hold of me that for several days I could not stop myself from repeating it to myself constantly," Simone wrote the following year. "At times the very first words tear my thoughts from my body and transport them to a place outside space where there is neither perspective nor point of view . . . filling every part of this infinity of infinity, there is silence, a silence which is not an absence of sound but which is the object of a positive sensation, more positive than that of sound."[15]

After her stay in the Alps, Simone spent a month working on the grape harvest with another family in the Ardèche, the Rieus, who gave her room and board in exchange for eight hours a day in the vineyards. She again refused to have a room of her own and slept on the floor of the Rieus' dining room, annoying her hosts by littering it with her papers. In addition to harvesting grapes she milked the cows at dawn, peeled vegetables and washed dishes in the evening, and of course insisted on helping the couple's children with their homework, as she did in every family with whom she lived. As for the daytime work, she found it hard to keep up with the harvesting, but persevered, often lying down on the ground when she was too tired to stand while continuing to pick the grapes. "Sometimes I'm crushed by fatigue," she admitted in a letter to a friend, "but I find in it a kind of purification. Right at the pit of my exhaustion I encounter joys that nothing else can give me."[16] The Rieus, in fact, were amazed that she could do a man's work while maintaining such a minimal diet. "We had to watch her like a hawk, for otherwise she would only have eaten very unnourishing food—onions, raw tomatoes. Her health seemed quite impaired, and she often had very bad headaches."[17]

Just before the end of the grape harvest, Simone wrote a barbed letter to Xavier Vallat, Vichy's Commissioner for Jewish Affairs, again emphasizing that she did not consider herself a Jew: "I . . . have never entered a synagogue, was brought up without any religious conviction whatever by free-thinking parents, have no attraction to the Jewish religion, no attachment to the Jewish tradition, and have been exclusively inspired since early childhood by the Hellenic, Christian, and French traditions." But this time she sharply protested the statute banning Jews from professorial jobs, ironically thanked her government for passing a recent edict that enjoined Jews to engage in manual work, and noted that she had obeyed the order by becoming a farmworker:

I look on the statute of Jews as generally unjust and ab-
surd. How can one believe that a university graduate in
mathematics could harm children who study geometry by
the mere fact that three of his grandparents attended a
synagogue? But in this particular case I would like to express my sincere gratitude to the government for remov-
ing me from the social category of intellectuals and giving
me the land, and, with it, all of nature.[18]

She looked forward to continuing her work as a farmhand
throughout the winter, on yet another job arranged for her by
Thibon. But at the last minute the farmer canceled his offer
to hire her, claiming that he could only employ people from
his own village. So, after returning to the Thibons for a few
days in late October, Simone rejoined her parents in Marseilles. And the following six months—the last ones she
would spend in France—were the most fruitful in her life as
a writer. The majority of the essays included in *Intimations
of Christianity* come from this period, as does much of the
long essay entitled "Forms of the Implicit Love of God." She
worked on her journals with unprecedented intensity, and
many of the entries from the twenty notebooks she filled in
Marseilles would be included in *Waiting for God,* the anthology of her writings Thibon edited after her death. She did
all this work while complaining to a friend in a letter that
she was succumbing to her "natural laziness."

All that winter Simone was again very active in the Resistance. Father Perrin put her in touch with a young schoolteacher, Malou David, who worked with the new underground
periodical *Cahiers du Témoignage Chrétien,* which represented left-leaning workers and was virulently opposed to
the Vichy government. It was a strictly clandestine publica-

tion, and soon Weil was in charge of its distribution in the entire Marseilles region. Weil and Malou David met almost every day, Weil acting as her colleague's letterbox and as her contact with the upper rungs of the Resistance chain. It was indeed a miracle that she was never arrested again: Her maladroitness was such that she once dropped a suitcase filled with Resistance documents, which lay scattered on the sidewalk of a busy street. In her memoir of Weil, Malou David notes that Simone insisted that if David were arrested, all responsibility should be attributed to Weil so that she—David—could be free to continue her work for the Resistance. The two women worked together until the day Weil left Marseilles, when she passed on to her colleague her large network of underground contacts.

During the last six months she was in France, Simone went to mass regularly on Sundays, and often went on to dine with the Honnorats, the Catholic couple who had introduced her to Father Perrin. After their long conversations she sometimes spent the night with them, insisting on sleeping on the rug next to her bed (they tried to thwart her by putting a lot of blankets on top of the rug). The issue at the forefront of her mind throughout this time was whether she was ready to become a Catholic: Before accepting Perrin's offer of baptism, she felt she must investigate the nature of the dogmas she would have to subscribe to. And she had to do this research tactfully, for she worried about hurting the feelings of the soft-voiced, nearly blind priest. "I can't enter the Church just to avoid causing him pain!" she wrote Thibon.[19]

It is in this context of search and indecision that Simone wrote the famous letters to Perrin the priest edited into her posthumous book, *Waiting for God.* These missives focus on her strong feelings of inadequacy. "Only those who are above a certain level of spirituality can participate in the sacraments," she writes him, emphasizing that she feels herself to be well below that level. Moreover, she is loath to separate herself from "the immense and unfortunate multitude of unbelievers." At a time of history when so large a proportion of humanity is steeped in materialism, she also wonders whether God might prefer that there be "some men and women who have given themselves to him and to Christ and who yet remain outside the Church." But her biggest stumbling block is the Church as social institution, and the "Church patriotism" that brutally excludes those who do not adhere to all its doctrines, and toward which she feels intense hostility. "I love God, Christ and the Catholic faith as much as it is possible for so miserably inadequate a creature to love them," she writes Perrin. "I love the Saints through their writings. . . . I love the Catholic liturgy, hymns, architecture, rites and ceremonies. But I have not the slightest love for the Church in the strict sense of the word."[20]

Throughout her letters to Perrin, Weil also repeats that she has not felt the call to baptism clearly enough. "If I had my eternal salvation placed in front of me . . . I would not put out my hand so long as I had not received the order to do so." But however rigorously and honestly she applied herself to her religious quest, one senses that she might have overlooked impulses anchored in a far deeper level of her consciousness. Might not her reluctance to join the Church have been equally impelled by her need to renounce all forms of satisfaction—by her spiritual anorexia? In this letter to Perrin, Weil herself makes a link between her dual impulses to physical and spiritual deprivation: "The relation of hunger to food is far less complete, to be sure, but just as real as is that of the act of eating. . . . It is not inconceivable that for a person of such innate dispositions . . . the desire for and deprivation of the sacraments might constitute a contact more pure than actual participation."[21]

The problem of "readiness for baptism" dominated Simone's conversation that winter, whenever she talked to a Catholic. While scrambling in the rocky hills above Marseilles with her friend Louis Bercher, she once solicited him to ask his sister, a very cultivated, knowledgeable nun, whether one could become a member of the Church if one believed that there was salvation *outside* it. The nun replied that in her view, such a belief was permissible, and the chaplain of her convent (which must have been ultraliberal) confirmed her opinion. Bercher relayed these conclusions, but Simone still remained insecure about them. "Please ask them again," she pleaded with her friend, "please, just to make sure." Bercher notes that Simone's anxieties about conforming with absolute precision to the teachings of the Church were part of the very authoritarian, conservative streak in her thinking. She considered Joan of Arc outrageous, and thought it perfectly right that she had been persecuted—where would we be if all young girls with strong opinions started imposing their political views? "I'm amazed that any of them are *allowed* to do that," she opined. She had a similar reaction when Bercher reported that his sister, the nun, felt she could talk to Christ "as to a friend." "I'm amazed they're *allowed* to do that," she said again, suggesting that his sister might have an overwrought imagination.[22]

At the end of March 1942, when she learned that she and her parents were about to obtain visas for North Africa and that she'd soon be forced to leave France, Simone went to spend Easter at the Abbey of En-Calcat, just northeast of

Carcassonne. She visited extensively with the poet Joë Bous-
quet, an authority on the Cathars and a frequent contributor
to *Cahiers du Sud* who had been severely crippled by a
World War I wound, and whose life she found a model of sto-
icism. She talked at length with a monk of En-Calcat, Canon
Fernand Vidal, to explore still further the issue of her readiness for baptism. Vidal gave her a far more negative reading
that had the Dominicans in Marseilles, and they generally
did not get along. "I found . . . in her spirit, something
crude, rigid and intransigent," Vidal noted, "[the same
traits] for which she reproached the Jewish people."[23]

Disappointed, Simone went on to discuss her problems
with yet another monk in the area, Dom Clément Jacob, to
whom she submitted a list of several issues she regarded as
obstacles to her entering the Church: Could one be baptized
if one believed that there were incarnations of the Word
prior to Christ—say, in Orphic mysteries, Chaldean and
Egyptian oracles, Taoist sages, Osiris, and Krishna? Of if one
believed that the knowledge of God given to non-Christian
persons in contemporary India was as genuine as the knowledge of God offered to Christians? Or if one wished to ban
the Old Testament from the canon of the Church? She presented dozens of such tenets that were dear to her, and the
response of Dom Jacob, who was irritated by what he
deemed to be her arrogance, was even harsher than all previous priests' had been: He told her in no uncertain terms
that such opinions were heretical. These encounters at En-
Calcat were turning points in Weil's spiritual life. Up to then
she had still thought there was a good chance for her to become a Catholic. After these confrontations she thought the
possibility was extremely distant.

Just before leaving Marseilles, Simone gave Father Perrin two of her most important essays, which he would also include in *Waiting for God:* "The Love of God and Affliction," and "Forms of the Implicit Love of God." As for Thibon, she saw him the day before she boarded the boat to Morocco. She handed him, very casually if not carelessly, a package of the twelve large notebooks in which she had kept her Marseilles journal, and which he would later edit into the book *Gravity and Grace.* "Soon there will be a distance between us," she wrote in the note she also handed him that day. "Let us love this distance, which is thoroughly woven with friendship, since those who do not love each other are not separated."

Simone sailed out of France with her parents on May 14, on a cargo ship that would take ten days to reach Casablanca. When Hélène Honnorat, seeing her off at the dock, said, "Au revoir in this world or the next," Simone answered, "No, in the next."

While awaiting passage to New York, the Weils were interned for seventeen days in a refugee camp on the outskirts of Casablanca. Simone slept on the cement floor of the room she shared with several other women, wrapped in blankets. She was fascinated by a group of Polish Orthodox rabbis who said their daily prayers in the vegetable garden, and impressed by the fastidiousness of their ritual tallith and phylacteries. Although it was her first time in a Muslim country, and she was an avid sightseer, she was so intent on finishing a commentary on Pythagorean texts that she left the camp only once, to see the wife of her friend Louis Bercher. Before mailing Perrin the essay on the Pythagoreans, she wrote him a long final letter in which she gently chided him for being "attached to the Church as to an earthly country." He had recently written her that the day of her baptism would be "a great joy" for him. She replied that she could not yet accept his church's notion of salvation, that "only God has the power to prevent me from giving you joy." To be truly "catholic" in the lowercase sense, she told him, we can not be "bound by so much as a thread to any created thing, unless it be to creation in its totality."[24] But she concluded on an affectionate note, telling him he would probably be able to popularize her thought far better than she herself ever could. In the same mail she also wrote to Hélène Honnorat, expounding on the sense of "laceration" she felt upon leaving French soil.

On June 7 the Weils finally left for the United States, on a Portuguese freighter called *Serpa Pinto*, which took an entire month to travel from Casablanca to New York. Simone refused the first-class cabin her parents had provided for her, insisted on traveling fourth class, and ended up sleeping on deck. She talked to almost no one onboard ship but an eighteen-year-old student, Jacques Kaplan (*"mon petit Jacques,"* as she addressed him), whom she appreciated because he was taking such excellent care of refugee children in the ship's hold. He would visit her often after they both reached New York, having found her "very pleasant, very protective, very sarcastic."[25]

10. New York

SHE HAD ALWAYS loathed the idea of coming to the United States, hated most things American. "[Americans'] hospitality is a purely philanthropic matter, and it is repugnant to me to be the object of philanthropy," she had written André while still in Marseilles. "It is more flattering . . . to be the object of persecution."[1] And no sooner had she arrived in New York than she started making plans to leave it. There is a mood of great desperation in the reams of letters she began to write within days of her arrival. They all focus on her need to get to London as soon as possible in order to take an active part in the war and be parachuted back into France.

She immediately wrote to the philosopher Jacques Maritain, who had settled in the United States the previous year, about her proposal for front-line nurses, enclosing a letter from Father Perrin that endorsed the plan (she even suggested that the influential Maritain might get her an interview with President Roosevelt!). She outlined the same project in a letter to Admiral Leahy, who had recently been recalled to Washington, and also to the future Gaullist minister Jacques Soustelle, who had arrived in London and whom she'd known at Normale. Of the numerous individuals to whom she penned entreaties concerning her need to get to London to carry out her project, the one in whom she had most faith (rightly, as it turned out) was Maurice Schumann, who was also in London with the Free French. Recalling the days when they had sat side by side at Alain's lectures, she appealed to his friendship to get her to England as soon as possible. Life was of no value to her, she told him, if she could not be "at the points of greatest danger." In another poignant missive she entrusted to a family friend, the future prime minister Mendès-France, she implored Schumann to see to it that once in London, she be sent to France to do liaison with the Resistance: "I beg you, get me over to London. Don't leave me to die of grief here. I appeal to you as a comrade."[2]

In the despair of those weeks, trying to adjust to a country she was clearly determined to detest, Simone even wrote a letter to a total stranger, a pro-French British officer she'd heard on the radio, asking his help in getting her assigned to a dangerous underground mission in France. "I would never have left France without the hope that through coming here I could take a greater part in the struggle, the danger and suffering of this war. . . . Now I find myself among comfort and security. . . . And I feel like a deserter. I cannot bear that. . . . My life is of no value to me as long as Paris . . . is subject to German domination."[3]

But as her brother, André, by then teaching at Haverford College in Pennsylvania, repeatedly tried to make clear to Simone, traveling from New York to London in 1942 was far more difficult than she had ever conceived. As a precaution against German attacks, ships, which were very few and in great demand, could only travel in convoys. Moreover, any French citizen needed three separate authorizations to get to Great Britain—from the British and U.S. governments, and also from the Free French headquarters. As this realization dawned on her Simone grew increasingly depressed. Her guilt about leaving her homeland had grown even deeper a few days after her arrival in New York, when she read in *The New York Times* that two women had been killed in Marseilles by Vichy policemen breaking up a Bastille Day demonstration. She started spending days on end on her sleeping bag, which she kept on the floor of her room, and during such withdrawals she could not be persuaded to take any food. "I can't go on living like this," she told her mother, adding that if the situation did not improve she would go to the south to work with blacks.

A few days after arriving in New York the Weil family had moved into an apartment at 549 Riverside Drive, between 123rd and 124th Streets (a plaque commemorating the dates of Simone's residence now designates the building). It had a sweeping view of the Hudson River, the George Washington Bridge, and Grant's Tomb; the military associations of the latter landmark depressed Simone further. In August she received her first letter from Thibon, and she immediately replied to elaborate on the guilt she felt about having left France. "The mere recollection of the streets of Marseilles and of my little house by the Rhône pierces my heart,"[4] she told him. In an attempt to allay her homesickness she spent hours on end at the Free French headquarters in Manhattan, needling officials to help her get a visa to England. A former secretary of those offices remembered her this way:

> She was very thin, very withdrawn, very reserved. She remained distant out of a sort of pride, as though she wanted to exorcise ill fortune by an apparent lack of interest. . . . [D]ressed with her usual indifference . . . she

rested her foot against the wall, knee bent, like some old sea dog. Her hair unkempt, glasses on her nose, cigarette in her mouth, she hid, under the mask of an expressionless face, the urge to get away that was consuming her.[5]

Simone's spirits were somewhat lifted by her pleasure in an important new friendship. Simone Deitz was a young Catholic convert, about her own age, whom she had met very briefly in Marseilles. Encountering her again at the Free French headquarters, she learned that Deitz, too, was desperately trying to get to England. When Weil asked Deitz, with her usual forthrightness, "Will you be my friend?" the two became inseparable. It was a friendship of contraries. Deitz was as exuberant, optimistic, and outgoing as Simone, at this point in her life, was withdrawn and moody. The two women took a first-aid course in Harlem, thinking the certificate might enhance their prospects of getting to London. Simone would often go to dinner at the Deitz home, occasions at which the Deitzes, appalled by her negligent diet, served steak, and at which her friend's father provoked her by declaring the superiority of Judaism over Christianity. While she was absorbed in the argument, he'd surreptitiously slip some additional meat on her plate, which she often ate.

Simone's output of publishable essays could not begin to be as prolific in New York as it had been in Marseilles. There were no French-language periodicals inciting her to work. Her spoken English was excellent, but her written English was less fluent, and the few articles she wrote in English—they were about racism, and she signed them with the pen name "Francis Brown"—were turned down. So she spent many hours at the New York Public Library, where she researched the affinities between Irish, Egyptian, and American Indian myths, and discovered the teachings of the Buddhist sage Milarepa. And she persevered in keeping her journal, filling more than three hundred often extraordinary pages in her four-month stay. Her New York writings are austere and bleak but informed by an admirable blend of mystical insight and social activism, two traits that seldom coexist in one religious thinker. "To die for God is not a proof of faith in God," so one journal entry reads. "To die for an unknown and repulsive convict who is a victim of injustice—that is a proof of faith in God."[6] Her deepening identification with the most deprived elements of God's creation permeates the dreadful prayer that follows, which was also found in her New York notebooks. Its ascetic repudiation of the flesh, which might be seen as an exaggerated reflection of Pascal's Jansenism, goes brutally beyond it:

Father . . . grant me . . . that I may be unable to will any bodily movement, or even any attempt at movement, like a total paralytic. That I may be incapable of receiving any sensation. . . . That I may be unable to make the slightest connection between my thoughts, like one of those total idiots who not only cannot count or read but has never even learned to speak. . . . May all this be stripped away from me, devoured by God, transformed into Christ's substance, and given for food to afflicted men whose body and soul lack every kind of nourishment. And let me be a paralytic—blind deaf witless and utterly decrepit. . . . Father . . . rend this body and soul away from me . . . for your use, and let nothing remain of me, forever, except this rending itself, or else nothingness.[7]

Once in New York, Simone also continued her relentless search for compatibility with the teachings of the Church. She objected fiercely to the notion that unbaptized infants go to hell, for instance. She started again to make her round of priests. Among the many clerics subjected to her grilling were Father Dietrich von Hildebrand, a noted theologian on the faculty of Fordham, and Father John Oesterreicher. She spoke to both about the superiority of Greek philosophy to the Old Testament as a precursor of Christianity, and her appetite for heretical arguments was not any more appreciated than it had been in France. They both tried to pass her on to yet other priests. "I wonder whether this new fellow will pass me on to yet another, and so on, until none of them are left," she wrote her parents while they were visiting André in Haverford.

Different learned priests gave her different answers, and she felt increasingly hampered in her journey toward Catholicism. But come September she began to see hope again when she met a very brilliant Dominican, Father Édouard Couturier, who had been recommended to her by Jacques Maritain. Her letters to him, written that fall, offer the most succinct summations available of her very complex positions on issues of faith. The priest so impressed her that although the young couple had no previous religious affiliations whatever, she recommended that Couturier prepare André Weil's ten-year-old stepson, Alain—Eveline Weil's son by her first marriage—for communion. In mid-September, Eveline gave birth to a daughter, Sylvie. Simone, who immediately adored the baby and gave her the bottle in surprisingly expert fashion whenever she came to visit, also wrote her brother lengthy letters arguing that Sylvie should be baptized in the

Church. André and Eveline Weil would follow both of her suggestions.

Notwithstanding her continuing frictions with Catholic doctrine, Simone, while in New York, went to mass almost daily at the Franciscan Church of Corpus Christi on 121st Street, a five-minute walk from her parents' apartment. Since she considered Latin a legacy of Roman imperialism, she much appreciated Corpus Christi's tradition of holding its liturgy in English, which at the time was considered very radical. On weekends she grew more ecumenical, and went regularly to a Baptist parish in Harlem and, much more rarely, to a small synagogue of Ethiopian Jews. The Baptist church service elated her. "The religious fervor of the Minister and the congregation explodes into dances much like the Charleston," she wrote her friend Dr. Bercher, "exclamations, shouts and the singing of spirituals . . . a true and moving expression of faith."[8]

In mid-September Simone finally saw some hope for her trip to England. The Free French organization in London had expanded considerably in recent months, and had greatly increased its contacts with the United States, which was preparing to invade North Africa. Maurice Schumann wrote Simone that he had spoken about her to André Philip, a former Socialist deputy who was now serving as commissioner of the interior in de Gaulle's provisional government, and that Philip, who was about to visit New York, favored bringing her over to London. In her long and grateful letter to Schumann, she insisted once more that any work she be assigned in London must involve a great deal of hardship and danger: "The suffering all over the world obsesses me and overwhelms me to the point of annihilating me, and the only way I can . . . release myself from this obsession is to take on a large share of danger and hardship myself. . . . I beseech you to obtain for me . . . the measure of hardship and danger that alone can save me from being wasted by sterile grief. . . ."[9]

Simone met André Philip a few weeks later, when he came to New York on the difficult mission of persuading Roosevelt to take a more positive attitude to the Free French. Their interview went so well that he offered her a job on his staff. This official invitation joyfully enabled Simone to prepare for her departure, which was set for November 10, when a convoy of five ships was scheduled to leave New York for London. But before leaving she had to clear up some political misunderstandings she was having with the French émigré community in New York. The French existentialist philosopher Jean Wahl, a Paris friend who now was also in London, wrote to tell her that she was rumored, among her émigré compatriots, to have pro-Vichy sympathies. She hastened to refute those accusations in a letter.

In her indignant denial she points out that the entire nation had welcomed the armistice and bore responsibility for the debacle of 1940: "All the French, including myself, are as much to blame for [the armistice] as Pétain . . . since then Pétain has done just about as much as the general situation and his own physical and mental state allowed him to limit the damage." And as she elaborates on the French tragedy, she expresses the first of several self-castigating mea culpas she will make on the issue: "Ever since I decided, after a very painful inner struggle, that in spite of my pacifist inclinations it had become an overriding obligation to work for Hitler's destruction . . . I've never swerved from my resolve . . . my decision was tardy, perhaps, and *I bitterly reproach myself for that.* But . . . since I adopted this position, I haven't budged."[10] (The italics are mine.)

As she prepared to leave, Simone also had to clarify, one last time, those difficulties with Roman Catholic doctrine that kept her from being taken into the Church. She needed a broad-minded priest to elucidate the vast differences she perceived between Church dogmatics as represented by "the catechism of the Council of Trent" and the original sources of Christianity—"the New Testament, the mystics, the Liturgy." And she decided to seek counsel from the man who had briefly served as her spiritual adviser in New York, Father Couturier. Her very long letter to Couturier—it went on for thirty-two manuscript pages, in tiny handwriting, on large seventeen-by-thirteen-inch sheets—was sent to him shortly before she left for Great Britain. Instead of querying him about points of Catholic doctrine, she began at the other end, and listed those of her beliefs she feared were heretical.

Her summary of her points of difference with the Church— set forth in thirty-five "heretical propositions"—focus on two principal themes. She first elaborates on her belief that divine revelation was just as fully embodied in the religions practiced in India, Babylonia, Greece, Egypt, Druid civilizations, and China long before the Christian Era; and, therefore, that such divinities as Osiris, Dionysus, Vishnu, Shiva, and Krishna had far more of "a share in God and Divine Truth" than Israel. In expounding on this aspect of her beliefs she again lashed out ferociously against missionaries ("a man's change of religion is as dangerous as a change of language for a writer") and excoriated the Church for cutting off Europe "from that antiquity in which all the elements of our civilization had their origins."

The second theme of Simone's letter to Couturier concerns her reasons for refusing the joys of baptism, and justifies her vocation as "a Christian outside the Church." She condemns Aquinas for having formulated the notion that faith is an intellectual assent to a set of interlinked propositions. Such a conception, in her view, involves "a totalitarianism perhaps more stifling than Hitler's," which is summed up by the odious words *anathema sit*, the phrase with which the Church branded texts and persons as heretical (she compares the institutional Church to the Nazi regime three times in the body of the letter). There is also a curious passage in Weil's letter to Couturier that greatly belittles the doctrine of the Resurrection: "If the Gospel totally omitted any reference to Christ's resurrection, faith would be far easier for me. The Cross alone suffices."[11] This is the only time, in Weil's voluminous writings, that she mentions the Resurrection (this central concept of Catholic doctrine was perhaps too joyful for her taste).

Despite Simone's fervent pleas, and her brother's, that they remain in the United States, Dr. and Mme Weil were doing all they could to follow her to Great Britain. But now that she had done her duty and saved her parents from Nazi persecution, Simone wished to follow the dictates of her own conscience, wherever they led her. She was determined that they not accompany her, and in this she was abetted by their inability to obtain the proper papers: Security about leaving the United States in wartime was very high, and only an official invitation from the Free French could get one to London. When their daughter left New York, Dr. and Mme Weil were not even allowed to go aboard ship, and had to say their last good-bye to her in an open shed that ran alongside the dock. Her parting sentence to her parents was: "If I had several lives, I'd have dedicated one of them to you, but I have only one life."[12]

Simone sailed out of New York on November 10, 1942, with ten other passengers, on a Swedish cargo freighter called the *Vaalaren*. Her friend Simone Deitz left for London in the same convoy, but on a different ship. As they were on the high seas the tide of World War II began to turn. Allied forces had landed in North Africa; the decisive battle for the Russian front had just begun at Stalingrad; in the following weeks Rommel would start to lose ground in the battle for El Alamein. And a day after Simone's departure from New York, Nazi forces swept into Vichy France. With the zealous help of Vichy police, which had already begun the task, they continued the roundup of Jews—large cities like Marseilles were particularly hard-hit—that would send some twenty-five thousand French citizens to their deaths in extermination camps.

11. London

IT TOOK TWO WEEKS to cross the Atlantic. One of Simone's fellow passengers, a British military man, recalls asking her why she ate so very little. She replied that she did not have the right to eat more than her compatriots in France; she was apparently persuaded that by some law of compensation the food she was refusing herself could become available to French children. She remained in high spirits, however, and emerged as the leader of the small band of passengers, keeping up their morale by gathering them on deck on clear moonlit nights and telling them folktales. After landing in Liverpool, the travelers were transferred to a screening center in the suburbs of London, known as "the Patriotic School," which was meant to detect spies in any group traveling to Britain. Here too she seemed to remain cheerful, learning to play volleyball and dressing up like a ghost to amuse her fellow inmates. The usual length of stay at the screening center was a few days, but she was detained for an entire fortnight because of her former left-wing affiliations. And she might have stayed far longer if Maurice Schumann, who now headed de Gaulle's information services, had not intervened to obtain her release.

Upon meeting with André Philip's deputy, Louis Closon,

who was responsible for liaison between Free French headquarters in Britain and Resistance groups in mainland
France, Simone suffered the first of many great disappointments she was to face in London: Her proposal for front-line
nurses was immediately and firmly turned down. ("But she
is mad!" de Gaulle is said to have exclaimed about the
"nurses project.") Her plan to be parachuted into France
with the Resistance was denied with equal firmness: She
would be too readily uncloaked, Closon told her, and might
place her comrades in danger. (It seems that Simone's "Se-
mitic" features, and her notorious physical maladroitness,
were also factors in the Free French's refusal to give her an
underground assignment.) These instant vetoes were big
blows to Simone; and recent news of Germany's occupation
of the Free Zone made her feel guiltier than ever about having left France at all. Instead of the heroic mission she had
dreamed of, she was appointed an editor in the civilian department, which was headquartered in Hill Street, and was
given a small office there.

For the first month of her stay in London, Simone was
billeted with the Free French women volunteers. But in
early January she found better lodgings on Portland Road,
near Holland Park, in the home of a cleaning woman of spir-
itualist leanings. The odd, reclusive boarder, who refused to
heat her room and said that she refused to eat because her
French compatriots were dying of hunger, soon came to be
beloved by the family. Her landlady, a Mrs. Francis, the
widow of a schoolteacher and mother of two sons aged fourteen and ten, immediately gave Simone an anthology of medieval mystics, *The Little Book of Comforts*. She described
her voice as being "ever so quiet and gentle," and found that

her face was the saddest she'd ever seen. On her part, Simone described the Francis household, in letters to her family, as "pure Dickens." She had an endless fund of stories to tell the Francis boys, whom she immediately started helping with their homework. They often left their school papers by her door to correct. And the younger Francis boy, whom Simone took to a Free French doctor when he was ill, became so attached to her that at times he curled up and went to sleep by her door, waiting for her to come home.

At first Simone's sorrow at being denied an underground mission was allayed by her great love for London. She agreed with T. E. Lawrence's portrait of the British, whom he had described as full of "humor and kindness." The British did not scream at one another as people did on the Continent, she wrote her parents, "they control [their temper] out of self-respect and from a true generosity towards others."[1] She was also impressed by the power of tradition in England, which she felt was part of the country's rootedness and strength, and found that the pub life in working-class districts was of a cloth with the drinking scenes in Shakespeare's plays. In her spare time she had many friends to see. She went to dine on weekends with the Closons and with the Rosins, German friends of her parents now living in London, whose son she tutored in mathematics. She enthusiastically attended performances of *King Lear* and *Twelfth Night*. She saw a great deal of Simone Deitz, to whom she taught some Tibetan in order that they might read Milarepa together. Deitz, on her part, tried to teach Simone how to drive, but gave up after one attempt—Simone had two small accidents within ten minutes. She often went to daily mass at the Jesuit church on Farm Street near her office, and on

Sundays she occasionally accompanied Schumann to the services at the Brompton Oratory in Knightsbridge, but left him at the door because she preferred to pray alone.

The Free French had two different offices in wartime London. The central headquarters, where de Gaulle reigned, were in Carlton Gardens, just off the Mall, in the former mansion, ironically, of Britain's virulently Francophobic nineteenth-century statesman Lord Palmerston. The "Interior Services," which André Philip directed and where Simone had her offices, were lodged in Hill Street, adjacent to Berkeley Square. The general character of the Free French organization was undergoing extensive change in the winter of 1942–43. In the previous two years of its existence it had concentrated on establishing its legitimacy with the rest of the Allies, which had proved difficult because of President Roosevelt's notorious hostility toward de Gaulle. But by the summer of 1942, as leading Socialists such as André Philip and Pierre Brossolette arrived in England, and as London headquarters' liaison with the mainland Resistance grew closer, de Gaulle also had to focus on securing his hold over the Resistance by accommodating its political interests.

In late 1942 the Free French underwent another important transformation that would greatly affect Weil's work in London. As victory became a distinct possibility, attention began to be given, both in London and in occupied France, to the principles on which a postwar France should be reconstructed. The patriots running the French Resistance were constantly communicating, to their counterparts in London, their views about the future postwar constitution, about the role of political parties, about a reformulated Declaration of the Rights of Man. Simone's job at Hill Street was to read, analyze, and respond to the reams of written material flowing from occupied France. She was no doubt highly sympathetic to most of the projects she read. Resistance leaders were not only rebelling against the Fascist nature of the Vichy regime. They were equally denouncing, as Simone had for years, the entire political ethos of the Third Republic, particularly the parliamentarism and party rivalry that they saw as responsible for the tragedy of 1940, and asking for a *tabula rasa*.

Weil's last and perhaps greatest work, *The Need for Roots*, written in the limbo between the Third and Fourth Republics, was her response to this historical crisis. Its principal thesis is that the Western nations' failure to fulfill the human need for roots was a central cause of the rise of totalitarianism in the twentieth century. The book runs radically against the mainstream of secular individualism, and begins with a thorough demolition of the fundamental ideal that has guided social theory since the eighteenth century— the centrality of human rights. This concept, in her view, is too tainted with egoistic self-interest, and leads to the positing of claims and counterclaims when different individuals' concerns come into conflict. She proposes that the notion of *rights*, which the Revolution of 1789 had turned into an absolute principle, must be exchanged for the notion of *obligations*, which she believes, somewhat like Kant, to be the only proper basis for morality. She also pinpoints one supreme "supernatural" duty that takes precedence over all other forms of commitments and is the cornerstone of her political and social vision: the obligation to respect every human being, an obligation that must be followed "for the sole reason that he or she is a human being, without any other condition requiring to be fulfilled . . . this . . . is the one and only obligation in the area of human affairs that is not subject to any conditions whatever."[2]

Weil then goes on to describe the different kinds of obligations nations must fulfill toward their citizens, in addition to the absolute obligation of human respect. She lists them in the form of antithetical pairs that are intended to be kept in perpetual balance. Here are a few of her pairings:

Liberty, which she defines as the privilege of always having the choice between many alternatives of action, and *obedience,* which must be freely consented to rather than based on punishment or reward.

Equality of respect and consideration, and *hierarchy,* which Weil defines as the human need for "a certain devotion towards superiors, considered not . . . in relation to the powers they exercise, but as symbols."

Honor and *punishment,* the latter of which—so goes her curious argument—should be regarded as a need rather than an imposition or correction, since "[M]en who are so estranged from the good that they seek to spread evil . . . can only be reintegrated with the Good by having harm inflicted upon them."

Security and *risk,* the first of which involves freedom from fear and harm; the second is dictated by our equal need for a playful variety of choices, a variety essential to avoiding boredom and heightening our courage.

Private property and *collective property.* In the network of decentralized, archaically small city-states Weil envisions as the ideal society, modest, individually owned residences are complemented by a large network of communal vegetable gardens, playgrounds, and civic centers. Her utopia excludes all state enterprises and giant private corporations.

Responsibility and *freedom of opinion.* The nature of the pairing, in this particular duality of Weil's "needs," is not clear. Responsibility involves our need to take part in decisions that affect "interests that are distinct from [our] own, but in regard to which [we] feel a personal concern." As for freedom of opinion, her thinking on the issue is so controversial that it needs special consideration.

Having taken a stand, in an early passage of *The Need for Roots*, for "unlimited freedom of expression for every sort of opinion," Weil goes on to state that the *individual's* freedom must be protected against "suggestion, propaganda, influence" that might be expressed by a *collective* group. "No group should be permitted by law to express an opinion . . . for when a group starts having opinions, it inevitably tends to impose them on its members,"[3] she states in this over-wrought passage, which is clearly influenced by her dread of the Nazi and Communist propaganda apparatuses, and also by the notion, widespread in Free French circles, that the press played an important role in the debacle of 1940. Should all statements on the part of political parties therefore be banned? How would elections be run? How could citizens give vent to those communal protests that are the essence of democracy? Should all media—the entire daily and weekly press—be subjected to this restraint? Weil never answers these questions and fails to define the precise nature of the "group-think" she would like to ban—a lack of specificity that has even led her to be accused of protofascist sympathies.

Weil is a passionate educator, and some of the principles she outlines for the education of youth in the postwar era can be as controversial as her views on curbing the freedom of the press. She believes that the young citizen's relationship to his society must be irradiated with a religious rather than political vision, for, as she puts it in a letter to Father Perrin, "the children of God should not have any country here below but the universe itself . . . that is the native city to which we owe our love."[4] For this purpose Weil demands the reintroduction of religion into all schools. In her view, it is the lack of a religious education—another legacy of 1789—that has made young people vulnerable to cults, drugs, violence, sexual license, and crime. But in Weil's lexicon "religious education," even if it were supplemented by a study of other major faiths, would still mean a predominantly Christian education. And in such passages Weil sounds uncomfortably close to our own Moral Majority or Christian right.

The Need for Roots is interspersed with long historical analyses of the "uprootedness" that led to the debacle of 1940, and lengthy digressions—alternately insightful and extremely eccentric—on French history (she traces the modern concept of the authoritarian state to Richelieu, and places great emphasis on the moral and intellectual degradation of the French elite that led to the defeat of 1940). It recaps all her favorite themes: combative distrust of most collective activities; antipathy toward Rome and love for Greece; the mistaken dominance given science in contemporary society; the need to imbue art and literature with moral values; the privileged role of physical labor; and the belief that liberty and equality are only genuine if infused with other worldly values.

Weil referred to *The Need for Roots* as "her second great work," along with *Oppression and Liberty,* and wrote her mother that she looked forward to her typing it out, as she had typed the earlier one. The two texts are indeed analogous. *The Need for Roots* retains the overriding concern with justice that informed *Oppression and Liberty;* but Weil's earlier emphasis on class struggle has given way to an emphasis on divine transcendence, and her passionate political concerns are now refracted through the prism of her religious experience. One might best describe the book as a vision of a Christian Socialist utopia that often fails as a concrete statement of aims but succeeds brilliantly as an indictment of the status quo.

The Need for Roots was only one small part of a huge body of work—some eight hundred manuscript pages of text—that Weil wrote in the five working months she spent in London (the rest of these writings are anthologized in a volume entitled *Ecrits de Londres*). The longest single paper she wrote for the Free French focuses on her proposal for the abolition of all political parties, and this fundamentally undemocratic concept has led some critics to complain that a France reconstructed on her lines would be somewhat similar to Vichy France, minus the collaboration with the Nazis, and with de Gaulle at the helm rather than Pétain.[5] Another controversial paper Weil wrote while in London concerned national policies to be taken toward "French Non-Christian Minorities of Foreign Origins," as Jews were sometimes referred to. In this instance the Resistance group to whose proposals she was reacting was of notoriously Fascist tendencies, and she feared that its members' demand for the official recognition of a segregated Jewish minority intended to create "a readily available reserve with a view to further atrocities."[6] But however benevolent Weil's intent, the unfortunate language in which she states her pleas for the total assimilation of Jews into French society has led to widespread misunderstandings: "The existence of such an [official Jewish] minority," she wrote, "does not represent a good thing; thus the objective must be to bring about its disappearance . . . official recognition of this minority's existence would be very unfortunate."[7]

Weil and de Gaulle never met face-to-face. And few of Weil's high-minded writings were ever seen by the general, who, given his own brand of protoreligious nationalism, his own tendency to commune with the mystical body of the nation—"I have *assumed* France," he once said—might well have been moved by their patriotic ardor. But the general, who was fiercely protected by his entourage, met very few of his junior colleagues on Hill Street. There is only one text of Weil's that de Gaulle is said to have read thoroughly, an essay written during her first weeks in London entitled "Reflections on Revolt." The national disgrace that had tainted France's image since 1940 was always uppermost in Weil's mind. This paper advocated the creation of a "Supreme Council of Revolt" that would project a more militant image of France's contribution to the Allied war effort by coordinating sabotage activities initiated in France with those programmed by the Free French in London. Weil's proposal might possibly have had some influence on the formation, in May 1943, of a National Council of the Resistance that would coordinate all diverse resistance groups in France and was headed by the great patriot Jean Moulin. Contrary to Weil's intentions, however, Moulin's National Council would be confined to activities on the French mainland; and to her horror, de Gaulle would insist that it include representatives of those same prewar political parties she believed had played a role in the nation's defeat.

The prolific pace of Weil's London writings took a terrible toll on her health. She kept to an exhausting schedule, seldom sleeping more than three hours a night. She often worked at her Hill Street office into the dawn hours, occasionally resting by putting her head down on her desk. She coughed more and more every week, but reassured her friends that her "smoker's hack" was caused by her ferocious chain-smoking. Her headaches had returned and grown far worse. She increasingly feared that she had actively collaborated in France's defeat by supporting, until the very brink of the war, a pacifist doctrine that had tragically failed. One of her letters from London refers to her "criminal error of pre-1939 days." When the young Frenchman she had befriended on her trip to the United States, Jacques Kaplan, arrived in London in March 1943 to join the Free French, he found her vastly changed from the energetic, ironic bluestocking he had known the year before. "She was worn out and tense, nerves stretched to a breaking point," he recalls. "[S]he seemed remote and it was impossible to make contact with her."[8]

In March 1943, increasingly tormented by her remorse over having left France at all, Simone Weil expressed her despair to Schumann. She felt misunderstood and totally rejected, and had great doubts as to whether her writings were being heeded by anyone in London. The work she was doing at Hill Street was "crippling [her thought]," she told him; it would soon be forced to a stop by her physical fatigue, and by "a moral limit . . . the ever increasing sorrow caused by the sense that I'm not in the right place."[9] In one of her last essays, "Theory of Sacraments," she drew a convoluted parallel between (1) the gulf between desire and reality joyfully bridged by Christ's presence in consecrated bread, and (2) the gulf (unbridged) between her sacramental desire to re-

Francine du Plessix Gray

turn to France and the dour reality of her situation in London. In other words she saw her longing for her homeland, and her passionate need to sacrifice herself to it, as sacred impulses the Free French were not allowing her to fulfill. "I am outside the truth," she moaned to Schumann. But the dear friend who had been able to get her to London could not get her to France. For all such underground missions were directed by a highly independent agency, the Bureau Central de Renseignment et d'Action, with which Schumann had no contact whatever. And when she appealed to a high-ranking officer of that organization, Jean Cavaillès, who spent much time working clandestinely in France and whom she had known at Normale (he was later shot by the Gestapo), he told her that the acts of noble, gratuitous heroism she proposed had no place in Resistance work.

Then she heard that the same Bureau Central had chosen her closest friend, Simone Deitz, to be parachuted into France. That was the last straw. She tried hard to convince Deitz—to no avail, of course—that she should take her place. Ultimately Deitz's mission was canceled, but the harm had been done: Simone felt more rejected, more out of place than ever. It is possible that she looked on her project of being parachuted into France as the most acceptable script for her death. She began to eat even less than before. Perhaps the clearest sign of her depression is that even the growing promise of an Allied victory, in the spring of 1943, offered her little joy. As her London colleagues rejoiced over the Russians' recent triumph over the German Sixth Army in Stalingrad and the Allies' definitive defeat of Rommel in Africa, she felt disgust at the petty rivalries and jockeying for position the prospect of victory had brought to the Free French.

And finally she collapsed. On April 15 Simone Deitz, failing to see her at the Hill Street office, went to her little room at Mrs. Francis's house on Portland Road. She found her lying unconscious on the floor. Upon being revived with a bit of brandy, Simone asked to telephone Maurice Schumann. She broke into tears as she spoke to him, saying, "It's all over now. I'll be taken to the hospital." She was brought to Middlesex Clinic, off Tottenham Court Road, where she was diagnosed with a granular form of tuberculosis in both lungs. The hospital staff immediately prescribed a more nourishing diet. But she refused to eat any more than she had before she fell ill, pleading that food rations in France, according to recent reports, had been further reduced. She got along well with the nurses but quarreled violently with the Middlesex doctors, who declared her to be the most difficult patient they had ever had to deal with.

Much of Simone's energy, from then on, would be devoted to hiding the truth from her parents, not allowing them to hear of her illness. She continued to mark her envelopes with her Portland Road address. Like all terminal anorexics, she seems to have thought increasingly about food. Her letters to her family, during those weeks of her hospitalization, are filled with references to delectable British fare—she was enjoying the London pubs more than ever, so she lied to them, she was filling herself with roast lamb and mint sauce, roast pork with applesauce, fruit fools. She worked for hours on one page of her letters home, managing to keep her handwriting steady so that her mother and father could not detect any change.

At first it was thought that Simone might be released from the hospital in two months, but the prognosis grew increasingly pessimistic. At the end of May the tubercular le-sions showed no improvement, and she continued to run a fever. After some weeks in the hospital she asked to see a priest, not because she desired baptism, she emphasized, but because she wished clearly to understand the obstacles to it. Simone Deitz brought the chaplain of the Free French, Father René de Naurois, to her bedside, and he visited her several times. Feverishly, not always coherently, she outlined for him the theological points she had listed some months earlier for Father Couturier, beginning with a query on the fate of nonbaptized infants.

Father de Naurois said that she spoke "rapidly and in a low voice, in sentences interspersed with silences," but grew far calmer when he had given her a blessing. The workings of her mind reminded him of "the acrobatics of a squirrel in a revolving cage." He described her in the following manner:

> I had the feeling of an extraordinarily pure and generous soul, to whom precisely because of its strength and rectitude the Lord had seemingly refused the tokens of Joy and Peace, preferring that she verify this truth unto the bitter end. . . . I had the powerful sense of a wholly docile, wholly ready soul that only escaped . . . through the subtleties of thought and analysis . . . [her thought] was highly abstract and abstruse, of a rapid dialectic, and very "feminine" . . . a thought that was elusive and at the same time prodigiously rich . . . which would not accept any fixed starting points from which to advance or retreat.[10]

At about the time that she received the chaplain's visits, Simone told her friend Simone Dietz: "If some day I'm completely deprived of will and in a coma, then I should be baptized." A few days later Deitz took some water from the tap, poured it on Simone's head, and pronounced the baptismal formula. *"Vas y, ca ne peut pas faire de mal,"* Simone said casually, "Go ahead, it can't do any harm."

Her will to live was being diminished by her extreme rage at the Free French. In the spring of 1943 de Gaulle's survival tactics were further complicated by the ascendance, on the new North African front, of the conservative and megalomaniac General Henri Giraud, whom the Americans named commander of French forces in Africa. In May, when de Gaulle, accompanied by his aides Schumann and Closon, left for Algeria to resolve his struggle with Giraud, Simone grew increasingly upset with the Free French. She loathed their politicking, and expressed fears that de Gaulle was forming his own political party. Some weeks later, shortly after the Allies had enhanced their strength by a successful landing in Sicily, she resigned from the Free French, stating her reasons for leaving the movement in a long and vehement letter to Closon. Since she had been refused any mission with the French underground, she wrote him, "I cannot have, and I do not wish to have, any direct or indirect or even very indirect connection with the French Resistance." In her postscript she added, "I am finished, broken, beyond all possibility of mending, and that independent of Koch's bacilli. The latter have only taken advantage of my lack of resistance and of course are busy demolishing it a little further. . . . The object may perhaps not be repaired but only temporarily glued together in such a way as to be able to function for a few more years. . . . Even a temporary gluing-together could only be accomplished by my parents, not by anyone else."[11]

Her beloved parents, that coddling, invasive couple who

up to now had always been on hand, always there to "glue her back together"—until the end she kept on fibbing to them about her life in London: the beauty of the early London summer, her favorite pubs, the Cockney ways of speaking; she asked for news of her little niece, Sylvie, and made plans for eventually rejoining them in North Africa.

With friends she was less accommodating. When Schumann came to see her at the hospital upon returning from Algeria, they had a violent argument. She reproached him for not trying hard enough to get her sent to France; she attacked his radio broadcasts for being too lenient with the Soviet Union and not exposing its Fascist regime; she went on to accuse him of the general degeneration of the Free French organization. She was not forbidding him to visit her again, she said, but she wished him to know that she would never speak to him again. And their very last meeting was indeed sadly silent. Upon entering her hospital room Schumann handed her a copy of *The Silence of the Sea,* a book by the Resistance leader Jean Vercors that had recently been published clandestinely in occupied France. She handed it back to him without even looking at it.

Not one of Simone's London friends—Schumann, Deitz, the Closons, the Rosins—felt that she wanted to die. She constantly talked about the future, about what she would do after France was liberated. And indeed, hers would not be any classical form of suicide, or even the kind of death many anorexics meet. Insofar as we can decipher any person's emotions at such moments, her attitude seemed to be one of apathy and detachment rather than active self-destruction. It is possible that she was not so much depriving herself of food as communing with her compatriots through abstention, not so much seeking death as cultivating that state of stoic indifference she had long admired. And it is probable that after years of increasing abstinence she had also developed a disorder of the digestive system that made eating very painful. What is harder to know is whether she realized with any degree of clarity the dangers she was running. Without having decided to die, she may not have fought hard enough against it.

From mid-July on, Simone had been asking to be transferred from Middlesex Hospital to a sanatorium in the country. According to her nurses, she was convinced that the fresh air would cure her. While anxiously waiting to hear whether her request would be fulfilled, she suffered several digestive attacks that further diminished her intake of food. In early August, in expectation of being moved, she supervised the packing of her books—Plato, the Bhagavad Gita, Saint John of the Cross. And she wrote a last letter to her parents, in which she continued her habit of using the English word "darlings": "Darlings—Very little time for letters now. They will be short, erratic, and far between; but you have other sources of consolation . . . au revoir darlings. Heaps and heaps of love."[12] In the past year she had been much consoled by the thought that the presence of her beloved little niece, Sylvie, was allaying her parents' anxiety about her.

On a Tuesday in mid-August she was finally transported, by ambulance, to Grosvenor Sanatorium, in the town of Ashford, in Kent. On arriving in her room she whispered, "What a beautiful room to die in." It was on the first floor, with a lovely view over wide lawns and fields. It faced south, and she immediately remarked that beyond the fields lay the sea, and France. How she rejoiced that her room looked toward her homeland! She ran a very high temperature. She had only one week to live.

Once again the sanatorium staff, and those of her friends who came to see her—Thérèse Closon, Simone Deitz—tried to make her eat. She made a great effort but could consume very little. She tried a few sips of champagne, but on most days her thoughts kept wandering back to the food of her youth. On Saturday, August 21, she took some spoonfuls of a French bread-and-butter soup she had asked for, and told Mme Closon that she might be able to eat some mashed potatoes, "You know, the kind my mother used to make." (One thinks of infants' pap, the kind of mush she was given as a baby during her chaotic crisis over mother's milk.)

On Sunday she ate an egg yolk with sherry, and even asked the sanatorium—by this time she may have been delirious—to hire a French cook. From then on, according to the nurses, she refused all foods because she feared she could not tolerate them. She may have been feeling great stomach pains. Throughout these last weeks in the hospital and the sanatorium, however, she continued to write in her journal, forcing herself to maintain a clear, strong hand. Excerpts from the last few pages of her journal:

> Blind man's stick. To perceive one's own existence not as itself but as part of God's will. . . .
> Think Christ with one's whole soul.—. . . Evil is not eliminated immediately in this way. But progressively it is. . . .
> A supernatural faculty.
> Charity.
> It is not, alas, conferred by baptism.[13]

And on these last days before her death she had sump-
tuous thoughts about the ritual importance of food:

> From the alliance between matter and real feelings comes
> the significance of meals on solemn occasions, at festi-
> vals and family or friendly reunions . . . (also sweets, del-
> icacies, drinking together . . .). And the significance of
> special dishes: Christmas turkey and candied chest-
> nuts—Candlemas cakes at Marseilles—Easter eggs—
> and a thousand local and regional customs (now almost
> vanished).
>
> The joy and the spiritual significance of the feast is
> situated *within* the special delicacy associated with the
> feast.[14]

"The eternal part of the soul feeds on hunger," she also
wrote during her last weeks. "When we do not eat, our or-
ganism consumes its own flesh and transforms it into energy.
It is the same with the soul. . . . The eternal part consumes
the mortal part of the soul and transforms it. The hunger of
the soul is hard to bear, but there is no other remedy for our
disease."[15]

The very last entry in her journal reads: "Nurses"

The word is spelled in English, with no punctuation.

Her vital signs remained fairly good on her last Sunday
and Monday, but weakened greatly thereafter. Tuesday, August 24, was a warm summer's day. At half past five in the afternoon she suddenly fell into a coma. Her heart stopped
beating at half past ten that evening.

The coroner's report, drawn up two days later, reads as
follows: "Cardiac failure due to myocardial degeneration of

the heart muscles due to starvation and pulmonary tuberculosis . . . the deceased did kill and slay herself by refusing to eat whilst the balance of her mind was disturbed."[16]

What a small, trifling part of it. She died of patriotism, out of sorrow and shame for the fate of France. She died of rage, because she wasn't allowed to do a man's heroic work. She died out of vengefulness, and, like all anorexics, out of a strong sense of spectacle. She, who since childhood had tended to take on the world's griefs, also died of remorse because she thought she'd collaborated in her nation's disgrace. She might have speeded her death through her loathing for her Jewish body, and her failure to acknowledge the deeply Jewish beauty of her mind. Historical circumstances not having allowed her to live like a good Cathar, she died like one, choosing the very way of death Cathars held up as the holiest. She died of something that might be called (depending on how you look at it) an illness—her pathological need to share the sufferings of others.

It's as simple as that.

She was buried three days later at the Bybrook Cemetery in Ashford, in a section that forms the border between the Jewish and Catholic sections of the burial ground. Among those standing at her grave that day were Simone Deitz; Maurice Schumann; her landlady, Mrs. Francis, and her two sons; and an old friend from her teenage years at Lycée Sévigné, Suzanne Aron, who had just arrived in London to join her husband, Raymond. A priest had been called for from London, but he missed his train because of an air raid alarm, so Maurice Schumann himself knelt down and read the prayers from his missal.

One can see Simone Weil's grave to this day in Bybrook

Cemetery. It can be hard to find, because there is no vertical slab marking it, only two horizontal markers, one of which records her dates: *"3 Février 1909   24 Août 1943."* However, over the years, her tomb has drawn so many visitors that the Ashford Tourist Bureau has printed maps of the cemetery that indicate the grave's location; upon the visitor's request it will even fax a copy to the information booth at the Ashford train station, where the Eurostar train (which links England with the Continent) now stops.

Simone's tomb, however, remains hard to detect because it is quite a bit to the right of the location marked on the tourist bureau's map. Look for the tall stand of yew trees at the very back row of graves and you will find it, fairly well tended, with a large ash tree just to the left of it, and, in late March, primroses and hyacinths growing haphazardly around the central slab, which says the following:

> *In 1942 Simone Weil joined the Provisional French Government in London, but developed tuberculosis and died in Grosvenor Sanatorium, Ashford.*
> *Her writings have established her as one of the foremost modern philosophers.*

Dr. Weil, who survived his daughter by twelve years, and Mme Weil, who died ten years after her husband, never had the heart to visit Simone's grave. But they commemorated her in another way: For the following many years they did little else but recopy her manuscripts for posterity. "It was like going to a job," their granddaughter Sylvie Weil says. "They sat down every morning and copied Simone's writings into neat black notebooks, and took a brief lunch break and copied again until late in the evening. They saw very few people beyond those who came to inquire about Simone. They were exclusively dedicated to the goal of preserving her work."[17]

Thus did Simone's parents continue to serve as an umbilical cord to reality, to a world this mystic did not seem able to survive without her mother and father at her side.

12. Our Father Who Art in Secret

_____

Simone Weil's philosophy crystallized into its final form during the last two years of her life. Here is a summation of some basic concepts that inform her work, and a sampling of the reactions they have elicited.

Creation and Decreation

God's act of creating the universe is one of renunciation and sacrifice. He must relinquish his status as sole power and reality in order to make space for other realities, must pull himself back, as it were, to give them room. "God could create only by hiding himself," so goes a jotting in *Gravity and Grace,* "otherwise there would be nothing but himself."[1] Since he is all goodness, God also has to renounce his power because power is opposite to goodness, and because he wishes us to obey him solely out of our own free will. This is a radically transcendent God who has tied his hands in the presence of evil, a suffering God who is torn asunder, separated from himself by human autonomy. It is only in the person of Christ, through Christ's crucifixion, that God can begin to be reunited with himself.

Weil's apposite concept of "decreation" has often been misread as evidence of her denigration of the physical world. In fact, it is something quite other, as her love of nature and of art, her intense involvement in social reform, and the following statement make clear: "For living man here below . . . sensible matter . . . is like a filter or sieve; it is the universal test of what is real in thought." So her "decreation" must be viewed, rather, in psychological terms, as a process of mimesis and return. Just as God, when he created the world, relinquished his power over us and the rest of nature, so we must relinquish the independence he offered us, and cease to live apart from him. In Weil's lexicon, there is a world of difference between "decreation," which she defines as "making something created pass into the uncreated," and "destruction," which entails "making something created pass into nothingness."

The language of paradox and contradiction familiar to all mystics abounds in Weil, and is made even more cryptic by her very terse aphoristic style. "God has created our independence to offer us the possibility of renouncing it out of love. . . . God in His love withdraws from us so that we can love Him. . . . He who has not God in himself can not feel His absence."[2] (At times, Weil's peekaboo deity resembles one of those nightmarishly perverse, sadistic lovers in French cinema who pepper their endearments with such conundrums as, "I must leave you in order to be with you.")

In her last years, influenced by the Upanishads and other Eastern systems of belief she was studying, Weil linked her concept of decreation to the notion that the self is an illusion that must be purged in order to find true contact with the Deity. Like many an earlier mystic, Weil often uses the concept of a screen—we must give up our own feelings totally enough to allow free passage, as through a transparent window, of God's love: "The self is only the shadow which sin and error cast by stopping the light of God. . . . The sin in me says I."[3]

But Weil's theology might be dictated by her spiritual anorexia as well as by Eastern influences. She does not allow herself any of the nourishing consolations—usually brought by some intimate contact with God—traditional to most mystics. "There are people for whom everything is salutary which brings God nearer to them. For me it is everything which keeps Him at a distance."[4] "If God becomes as significant to us as treasure is to a miser, we must tell ourselves that he does not exist. . . . We must prefer real hell to an imaginary paradise."[5]

Seldom does she phrase her impulse to self-annihilation more brutally than in the following sentence, written to the Dominican priest Father Couturier: "When I think of the Crucifixion, I commit the sin of envy."[6]

Necessity and the Created World

The world of space and time is the terrain in which God's most precious gift to man, free will, is acted out. It is dominated, alas, by Necessity, those inflexible laws of nature and history whose often brutal expression—wars, pestilence, the suffering of innocents—we have always struggled to reconcile with God's goodness. Our only path to spiritual illumination (here Weil is at variance with Manichaeism) is through a serene acceptance of the mechanism of Necessity. We must accept it as just and beautiful, we must even admire it, we must practice what the Stoics called *Amor fati*, a calm acquiescence to nature's most brutal laws, and of our utter insignificance in relation to the cosmos. However pitiless and implacable these laws, "as blind and exact as the laws of gravitation," we must love them because they are expressions of God's will.

By meditating on Necessity's indifference to us (one of the last phrases of Camus's *The Stranger, "la tendre indifférence du monde,"* might well have been influenced by a reading of his beloved Simone Weil) we can cultivate a true detachment from material creation. Only this experience of detachment, of acute voidness—the *via negativa* of medieval mysticism—might create interstices through which God can enter and touch us. "Grace fills empty spaces . . . it can only enter where there is a void to receive it, and it is grace itself which makes this void."[7] "Only when man accepts the void can grace rush in." Yet another cryptic Weilian aphorism: "The world is a closed door. It is a barrier. And at the same time it is the way through."[8]

The bitter experience of our insignificance and of God's infinite distance from us—echoes of Pascal's vision of God as the Totally Other—are of central importance to Weil. It is only through painfully feeling his absence that we begin to experience his presence. "God and the supernatural are hidden and formless in the universe. It is well that they should be hidden and nameless in the soul."[9] "We must experience the fact that we love him, even if he does not exist."[10] "A method of purification: to pray to God . . . with the thought that God does not exist."[11] (One possible interpretation: Since God does not exist in the same way as the created things we apprehend with our natural faculties, supernatural reality might first be experienced as nothingness.)

In a passage eerily precursive of the "Death of God" theology that would arise in the postwar years, Weil also compares the emotions we feel toward God to our emotions toward the dead: "The presence of the dead person is imaginary, but his absence is very real; henceforth it is his way of appearing." She illustrates this point—this is one of her favorite rhetorical devices—with an example from classical Greek drama. Just as Electra "preferred the absence of Orestes to the presence of anyone else," so we must love God, who is absent from material creation, more than any object in it.[12]

But what kind of a love of God are we pitiful creatures capable of? This is what Weil examines in her pivotal essay, "Forms of the Implicit Love of God."

The Implicit Love of God

There are three potential objects of human love in which God is secretly present, and through which we can therefore love him in an indirect or implicit manner: love for our neighbor, for religious rituals, and for the order and beauty of the created world. These implicit or "veiled" loves constitute a stage through which we must absolutely pass in order to reach the explicit contact with God that only the most privileged mystics attain: "The soul is not ready to receive the personal visit of its Master, unless it has in it all three indirect loves to a high degree. . . . The veiled form of love necessarily comes first and often reigns alone in the soul for a very long time. . . . Veiled love can reach a very high degree of purity and power."[13]

The love of our neighbor has to do with our absolute compassion for every human being, and, above all, with justice, that most sacred of principles, which is exclusively based on mutual consent. Justice—another mimetic principle that emulates the workings of divine compassion—is always a pivotal point of Weil's ethics: "He who treats as equals those who are far below him in strength really makes them a gift of the quality of human beings. . . . As far as it is possible for a creature, he reproduces the original generosity of the Creator.[14] . . . The supernatural virtue of justice consists of behaving exactly as though there were equality when one is the stronger in an unequal relationship."[15]

Another form of "veiled" or "implicit" love of God that draws us nearer to him is our love for religious practices. Like Pascal, Weil holds prayer in the greatest importance, and believes that the practice of rituals can help us to deepen our faith. "The recitation of the name of the Lord," she writes, "truly has the power of transforming the soul." But in terms of Roman Catholic doctrine, Weil verges far more closely on heresy than Pascal ever did. If practiced with a pure heart, rituals of all the major faiths, she insists, have the same sacred power, and can bring redemption to whomever performs them "with desire." (One can imagine how such a universalist view was received by the stern Dominican monks of Provence with whom she held her last theological discussions in France.) It is also in this passage that Weil lashes out ferociously against Roman Catholics' zeal for converting those born into other faiths. She is severely opposed to conversion, for the religion of one's birth, she esteems, serves as "a ladder" from which one can best grasp the beauty of other faiths. "We must have given all our attention, all our faith, all our love to a particular religion in order to think of any other religion with the high degree of attention, faith and love that is proper to it."[16]

The third "implicit" form of loving God designated by Weil—our obligation to love "the beauty of the world"—is such an essential facet of her thought that it is considered separately below.

Beauty

The beauty of the world displays "the cooperation of divine wisdom in creation." It is a sacramental quality which "like a mirror . . . sends us back to our desire for goodness." Whereas the achievements most of us mistake for ends— money, power—are merely means, beauty alone is a good in itself, and can never be a means to anything else. As Kant perceived, it is "a finality which involves no objective."[17]

It is also through the world's beauty that brute necessity most readily becomes an object of love. Here again, Weil is antiascetic. With the exception of Saint Francis, whose life she looks on as "perfect poetry in action," she repeatedly castigates Christianity's lack of emphasis on nature's physical splendor. Our very longing for the beauty of the world, in her view, is God-inspired. It is part of our yearning for the Incarnation. It is eternity here below. It also has a deep ethical dimension, a view elaborated in Weil's play *Venice Is Saved,* in which the hero commits treason against his own state—the Spanish Empire—to save the city, which has captivated him through its beauty and valor.

Beauty, of course, is the bridge to art, which is "an attempt to transport into a limited quantity of matter, molded by man, an image of the infinite beauty of the entire universe." Predictably, Weil's views of art are utopian, rigorously traditional, and somewhat priggish, and she would probably have been appalled by most contemporary aesthetic artifacts, based as they are on shock and information value rather than on traditional notions of "Beauty" with a capital *B*. She believes that works of art that are not "true reflections of the beauty of the world" have little validity, and that every true artist has a real, direct, and immediate contact with the world's beauty, "a contact that is of the nature of a sacrament."[18]

Affliction

At the time of her first religious experiences Weil began to differentiate between *la douleur,* physical suffering, and *le malheur,* a more psychological term that is best translated as "affliction." Unless it is chronic and severe—such as the pain caused by Simone's headaches, which might indeed turn it into affliction—physical suffering is a transient state that we usually learn to bear until it disappears, and that does not leave any permanent marks. (Weil points out that even severe emotional pain, such as sorrow over the loss of a loved one, can be healed or at least diminished over time.)

Affliction, on the other hand, is a profound distress of both body and spirit that leaves permanent marks on our bodies *and* our souls. It involves humiliation and social degradation of the kind that she saw being branded, during her months on the production line, on factory workers. In such excessive instances as slavery, "an extreme form of affliction," victims are even deprived of their personalities and reduced to objects.

Job, of course, is a perfect example of affliction. One of Weil's most subtle points is that the kind of affliction suffered by Job stamps our souls with "the sorrow, the disgust, and even the guilt and defilement that crime logically *should* produce but actually does not . . . everything happens as if the state of soul is criminal."[19] It is these feelings of guilt, of abasement, and even, in particularly acute moments, of criminality that seem to have been innate to Simone Weil since her youth, and may have enabled her to identify so deeply with the wretched of the earth.

However, affliction, this "marvel of divine technique," plays an important role in our eventual illumination. It is also through suffering that the world's beauty can reach us, since "suffering alone gives us contact with that necessity which constitutes the order of the world."[20] (Throughout her writings on affliction, one is struck by Weil's kinship to Kafka, who wrote that "[c]ontradiction is our wretchedness, and the feeling of our wretchedness is the feeling of our reality . . . that's why we must love it." To both writers, the transforming power of suffering is indispensable to understanding that the entire universe is "the vibration of the word of God.")

Attention and Waiting

Weil's thoughts on attaining a state of grace are best expressed in her own words, with little commentary.

> We must not want to find: as in the case of an excessive devotion, we become dependent on the object of our efforts. . . . It is only effort without desire (not attached to an object) which infallibly contains a reward. . . . By pulling at the bunch, we make all grapes fall to the ground. . . .[21]
>
> Attention consists of suspending our thought, leaving it detached, empty and ready to be penetrated by the

object. . . . Above all our thought should be empty, waiting, not seeking anything, but ready to receive in its naked truth the object which is to penetrate it. . . . We do not obtain the most precious gifts by going in search of them but by waiting for them. . . . This way of looking is, in the first place, attentive. The soul empties itself of all its own contents in order to receive the human being it is looking at, just as he is, in all his truth. Only one who is capable of attention can do this. . . .

The wrong way of seeking: the attention fixed on a problem. Another phenomenon due to horror of the void. . . .

The attitude that brings about salvation is not like any form of activity. The Greek word which expresses it is υπομενή, and *patientia* is rather an inadequate translation of it. It is the waiting or attentive and faithful immobility that lasts indefinitely and can not be shaken. The best image for it is that of the slave who waits near the door so as to open as soon as the master knocks. He must be ready to die of hunger and exhaustion rather than change his posture. . . . Even if he is told that the master is dead, and even if he believes it, he will not move.[22]

In our acts of obedience to God we are passive; whatever difficulties we have to surmount . . . there is nothing analogous to muscular effort; there is only waiting, attention, silence, immobility, constant through suffering and joy. The crucifixion of Christ is the model of all acts of obedience.

This kind of passive activity, the highest of all, is perfectly described in the Bhagavad-Gita and in Lao-Tse. . . .

As Aeschylus says: "There is no effort in what is divine." There is an easiness in salvation which is more difficult to us than all our efforts.[23]

So there is little we can do to attain faith, or redemption, or most good things Weil wants for us. The greatest quarrel she has to pick with Pascal, in fact, concerns his notion that we should actively pray for grace. On this issue Samuel Beckett might have understood her meaning better than anyone else: We can do little else than wait, little else than maintain a degree of acutely loving attentiveness to the living world. Or as we used to say in the antiwar movement (which, as Staughton Lynd notes, much appreciated Simone Weil) when advocating civil disobedience: "Don't just *do* something, *stand* there."

Food, Sacred and Profane

Metaphors of food and hunger recur throughout Weil's writings to an obsessional degree, and are often imbued with a very negative view of the act of eating.

> My meat is to do the will of Him who sent me. . . .
> Friendship is a miracle by which a person consents to view from a certain distance, and without coming any nearer, the very being who is as necessary to him as food. . . .
> The beautiful is a carnal attraction which keeps us at a distance and implies a renunciation. . . . We want to eat all the other objects of desire. The beautiful is that which we desire without wishing to eat it. We desire that it should be.[24] [Does she view eating as a form of original sin?]

Weil was so fond of this paradigm of looking/eating that she repeated it in her journals and her letters, and the metaphor eventually made its way into different books: "The great trouble in human life is that looking and eating are two different operations. . . . It may be that vice, depravity and crime are nearly always, or even perhaps always, in their essence, attempts to eat beauty, to eat what we should only look at. Eve began it."[25] (Might this mean that paradise, for Weil, would be a condition in which she would be forever allowed to sate her appetite?)

"The beauty of the world is the mouth of a labyrinth. The unwary individual who on entering takes a few steps is soon unable to find the opening . . . if he goes on walking, it is absolutely certain that he will finally arrive at the center of the labyrinth. And there God is waiting to eat him."[26]

From a letter to Father Perrin: "My situation with regard to you is like that of a beggar, reduced by extreme poverty to a state of constant hunger, who for the space of a year had been going at intervals to a prosperous house where he was given bread."[27]

One should keep in mind that the female mystic's rendering of supernatural experience is traditionally imbued with eroticized images of food and lactation. To Julian of Norwich, "our precious Mother, Jesus . . . can feed us with a substance far more precious than mother's milk, Himself." Clare of Assisi, an anorexic who from her early youth slept on wooden boards and secreted her food away to the poor, had dreams that she suckled at the breast of her hero, Saint Francis of Assisi. To another anorexic saint, Teresa of Avila, the Lord's kiss was also "sweeter than wine."

"A child does not stop crying if we tell him that there is no bread . . . it goes on crying all the same. The danger, for the soul, is not to doubt whether there is any bread, but to persuade itself, through lying, that it is not hungry."[28]

Might Weil have been all the more attracted to Christianity because of its obsessive emphasis on food, because of the cannibalistic associations of Holy Communion? "At the center of the Catholic religion a little formless matter is found, a little piece of bread . . . a fragment of matter. . . . Herein lies the great scandal and yet the most wonderful virtue of this religion."[29]

After Simone

Within two decades after her death, T. S. Eliot had written that Simone Weil, although she displayed "an almost superhuman humility and what appears to be an almost outrageous arrogance," possessed "a kind of genius akin to that of the saints."[30]

The French Existentialist philosopher Gabriel Marcel objected that "the agonizing voice of this practically dejudaised Jewess" was "refractory to hope."[31]

To Graham Greene, Weil stood "at the edge of the abyss, digging her feet in, refusing to leap like the common herd (whom she loved in her collective way), demanding that she alone be singled out by a divine hand on her shoulder forcing her to yield."[32]

The American critic Leslie Fiedler wrote that she symbolized "the Outsider as Saint in an age of alienation."[33]

American lay theologian Doris Grumbach accused her of manifesting an "almost Protestant pride" for refusing a mediator between herself and God.

To Alfred Kazin, the greatest gift offered by Weil, "a fanatically dedicated participant in the most critical experiences of our time," was the following: She remained "remarkably open to all human experience at its most extreme, neglected, and uprooted. . . . What she sought more than anything else was a loving attentiveness to the living world that would lift man above the natural loneliness of existence."[34]

Kenneth Rexroth referred to *The Need for Roots* as "a collection of egregious nonsense surpassed only by the deranged fantasies of the chauvinist Péguy," and accused Weil of "a captious, misinformed playing with Hinduism and comparative mythology, worse than the confabulations of Robert Graves."[35]

"Why could Simone Weil believe in a God of love and grace only through converting the God of the Jewish people into an incarnation of Satan?" asked the Jewish theologian Hans Meyerhoff. "*The Notebooks* reveal that she inflicted this deep wound upon herself and committed the slander against her own people as a last desperate measure of defense against total despair."[36]

The winner of the 1980 Nobel Prize for Literature, Czeslaw Milosz, who in the late 1950s translated Weil's selected works into Polish, believed that "[s]he has instilled a new leaven into the life of believers and unbelievers by proving that . . . many a Christian is a pagan, many a pagan is a Christian in his heart," and that "her intelligence, the precision of her style, were nothing but a very high degree of attention given to the sufferings of mankind." The reason why she fascinates so many in our time, he ventures, is that we live in an age "with a marked bias for Manichaeism"; she particularly resonates in our times, he adds, because our literature is marked by "a rage directed against a world which no longer seems the work of a wise clockmaker."[37]

The Irish historian and critic Conor Cruise O'Brien censured Weil's last book, *The Need for Roots*, for encouraging "a rigid, primitive, and eccentric form of censorship—one which would permit Jacques Maritain to be punished for having said something misleading about Aristotle."[38]

Susan Sontag wrote that Weil exemplifies the culture heroes of our age, who are both antiliberal and antibourgeois, who are "repetitive, obsessive, and impolite, who impress by force—not simply by their tone of personal authority and by their intellectual ardor, but by the sense of acute personal and intellectual extremity." Through Weil, she adds, the modern reader can "pay his respect to a level of spiritual reality which is not, could not be, his own."[39] So Weil, Sontag intimates, serves as a kind of scapegoat for our unfulfilled impulse to virtue and purity: She goes further than any of us would dare to venture, *she does it for us.*

Albert Camus spent an hour of meditation in her Paris room before boarding the plane to Stockholm to accept the Nobel Prize.

Pope Paul VI is said to have looked on Bernanos, Weil, and Pascal (the last of whom also died young, at the age of forty-one, before he could complete his *Pensées*) as the three most important influences on his intellectual development.

Simone Weil has been praised and condemned, commented, annotated, interpreted, footnoted, almost to extinction. But to my knowledge, no critic has fully elucidated the meaning of the following fable, which she wrote in Marseilles shortly before leaving for the United States, and which she entitled simply "Prologue."[40]

Prologue

He entered my room and said: "Poor creature, you who understand nothing, who know nothing. Come with me and I will teach you things which you do not suspect." I followed him.

He took me into a church. It was new and ugly. He led me up to the altar and said: "Kneel down." I said: "I have not been baptized." He said: "Fall on your knees before this place, in love, as before the place where lies the truth." I obeyed.

He brought me out and made me climb up to a garret. Through the open window one could see the whole city spread out, some wooden scaffolding, and the river, on which boats were being unloaded. The garret was empty, except for a table and two chairs. He bade me be seated.

We were alone. He spoke. From time to time someone would enter, mingle in the conversation, then leave again.

Winter had gone; spring had not yet come. The branches of the trees lay bare, without buds, in the cold air full of sunshine.

The light of day would arise, shine forth in splendor, and fade away; then the moon and the stars would enter through the window. And then once more the dawn would come up.

At times he would fall silent, take some bread from a cupboard, and we would share it. This bread really had the taste of bread. I have never found that taste again.

He would pour out some wine for me, and some for himself—wine which tasted of the sun and of the soil upon which this city was built.

At other times we would stretch ourselves out on the floor of the garret, and sweet sleep would enfold me. Then I would wake and drink in the light of the sun.

He had promised to teach me, but he did not teach me anything. We talked about all kinds of things, in a desultory way, as do old friends.

One day he said to me: "Now go." I fell down before him, I clasped his knees, I implored him not to drive me away. But he threw me out on the stairs. I went down unconscious of anything, my heart as in shreds. I wandered along the streets. Then I realized I had no idea where this house stood.

I have never tried to find it again. I understood that he had come for me by mistake. My place is not in that garret. It can be anywhere—in a prison cell, in one of those middle-class drawing-rooms full of knick-knacks and red plush, in the waiting-room of a station—anywhere, except in that garret.

Sometimes I cannot help trying, fearfully and remorsefully, to repeat to myself a part of what he said to me. How am I to know if I remember rightly? He is not there to tell me.

I know well that he does not love me. How could he love me? And yet deep down within me something, a particle of myself cannot help thinking, with fear and trembling, that perhaps, in spite of all, he loves me.

Acknowledgments

My first and foremost debt is to Florence de Lussy, curator of the Simone Weil archives at the Bibliothèque Nationale de France, who has been my principal source of guidance in the writing of this biography. I thank Mme de Lussy for the gracious generosity and warmth with which she put her documents, her wisdom, and her time at my disposal, and for the enthusiasm and encouragement she unfailingly displayed toward this project.

Special gratitude to my friend Pierre Nora, who initially put me in contact with Mme de Lussy and with the editor in charge of the Gallimard edition of Weil's collected works, Françoise Sibielle. And profound thanks to Sylvie Weil, whose great generosity in sharing family memories with me, and in allowing me to access her photographic archives, has been of invaluable help.

Equal gratitude to my friend George Lechner, whose help with every phase of my research was most precious to me; and to Jonathan Fasman, whose ability to compose perfectly computerized notes is coupled with an ear for finely tuned prose that is equivalent to a musician's perfect pitch.

I also give thanks to those family members, friends, and scholars who took time to read and annotate my text in manuscript form: Cleve Gray, who throughout my nine published books has remained my most astute and industrious critic; Luke Gray, an equally scrupulous critic-in-residence; my angelic reader Claire Bloom; Professor David

Acknowledgments

Schalk of Vassar and Professor David Levering Lewis of Rutgers, superb scholars who gave my text the kind of rigorous historical perusal every biographer dreams of. And loving thanks to my beloved friend of many decades Gabrielle Van Zuylen, who has sheltered, fed, and nurtured me during my research trips to France, and whose sisterly love and generosity have been a great source of strength throughout my life.

A few reflections on my translation process: When citing passages in Weil's writings from Simone Pétrement's majestic biography of the author, I've often based my renderings on the American edition published in 1976; but I've frequently referred to the far more complete French edition when I felt the translations were awkward or ill-tuned. The same principle guided my use of citations from Weil's major works: *Waiting for God, Gravity and Grace, The Need for Roots,* the *Notebooks.* Looking on endnotes as a community service of sorts, I've indicated the English-language sources of the direct quotations but have often refined them by consulting the original French texts.

To do justice, in some two hundred pages of text, to the legacy of a mind as complex and diffuse as Simone Weil's—a mind that delved with equal agility and brilliance into politics and spirituality, history and ethics, poetics and psychology—has been a demanding task. My principal goal was to heighten our understanding of the personal and social pressures that confronted this visionary thinker during her thirty-four years of life. To fulfill this aim I've tried to delineate the principal features of her character and of her thought—her asceticism, her quest for spiritual purity and martyrdom, her striking insights into domination and oppression—by setting them into the context of her unusually intricate family relations, and of the socio-historical conditions of France between the two world wars.

Notes

1: The Factory of Genius

1. André Weil, *André Weil: The Apprenticeship of a Mathematician,* translated by Jennifer Gage (Basel/Boston/Berlin: Birkhäuser Verlag, 1992), p. 16.

2. Jacques Cabaud, *Simone Weil: A Fellowship in Love* (Des Moines and New York: Channel Press, 1964), p. 19.

3. Simone Pétrement, *Simone Weil: A Life,* translated by Raymond Rosenthal (New York: Pantheon, 1976), p. 7.

4. Ibid., p. 13.

5. Alexandre Alder and Bernard Cohen, *Juif et Juif* (Paris: Éditions Autrement, 1985), p. 39.

6. Ibid., p. 37.

7. Gabriella Fiori, *Simone Weil: An Intellectual Biography,* translated by Joseph R. Berrigan (London and Athens: University of Georgia Press, 1989), p. 24.

8. Ibid., p. 15.

9. Ibid., p. 16.

10. Ibid., p. 20.

11. Ibid., p. 19.

12. Simone Weil, *Waiting for God,* translated by Emma Craufurd (New York: Harper Perennial Library, 1951), p. 64.

13. Pétrement, *A Life,* p. 28.

14. Fiori, *An Intellectual Biography,* p. 26.

15. Pétrement, *A Life,* p. 26.

2: The Master Teacher

1. Fiori, *An Intellectual Biography,* p. 28.

2. Pétrement, *A Life,* p. 34.

3. Fiori, *An Intellectual Biography,* p. 40.

4. Pétrement, *A Life,* p. 45.

5. Fiori, *An Intellectual Biography,* p. 58.

6. Simone Pétrement, *La Vie de Simone Weil* (Paris: Librarie

Notes

Arthème Fayard, 1973), p. 59
(hereafter referred to as
"Pétrement, French edition").

7. Ibid., p. 60.

8. Cabaud, *A Fellowship in Love*, p. 28.

9. Registers of Lycée Henri IV, cited in Pétrement, *A Life*, pp. 41–42.

10. Fiori, *An Intellectual Biography*, p. 38.

3: "Normale"

1. Simone de Beauvoir, *Memoirs of a Dutiful Daughter* (New York: Harper & Row, 1974), p. 243.

2. Pétrement, *A Life*, p. 59.

3. Fiori, *An Intellectual Biography*, pp. 57–58.

4. All of Lecarpentier's citations are from ibid., p. 48.

5. Fiori, *An Intellectual Biography*, pp. 41–42.

6. Pétrement, *A Life*, p. 58.

7. Fiori, *An Intellectual Biography*, p. 46.

8. Ibid., p. 49.

9. Pétrement, *A Life*, p. 69.

10. Pétrement, French edition, p. 116.

11. Ibid., p. 119.

12. Ibid.

13. Ibid., p. 70.

14. Cabaud, *A Fellowship in Love*, p. 43.

4: The Militant Years, 1931–34

1. David McLellan, *Simone Weil: Utopian Pessimist* (London: Macmillan, 1989), p. 39.

2. Pétrement, *A Life*, p. 78.

3. Simone Weil, "La Vie Syndicale: En marge du Comité d'études," *L'Effort*, December 19, 1931.

4. Pétrement, *A Life*, p. 131.

5. Ibid., p. 176.

6. Ibid., p. 181.

7. Ibid., p. 190.

8. Ibid., p. 182.

9. *Laure: Une Rupture*, edited by Jérôme Peignot, and Anne Roche (Paris: Éditions des Cendres, 1999).

10. Simone Weil, *Oeuvres Complètes*, vol. 6 (Paris: Gallimard, 1994), p. 132.

11. Ibid., p. 138.

12. Pétrement, *A Life*, p. 201.

13. Ibid., p. 209.

14. Georges Bataille, "La Victoire militaire et la banqueroute de la morale qui maudit," *Critique* 40 (September 1949), cited in Weil, *Oeuvres Complètes*, vol. 6, p. 1252.

15. Simone Weil, *Oppression and Liberty*, translated by Arthur Wills (London: Routledge & Kegan Paul, 1958), pp. 75–76.

16. Ibid., p. 69.

17. Ibid., p. 85.

18. Ibid., p. 124.

19. Weil, *Oeuvres Complètes,* vol. 1 (Paris: Gallimard, 1991), p. 329, cited in McLellan, *Utopian Pessimist,* p. 91.

20. Albert Camus, introduction to Weil, *Oeuvres Complètes,* vol. 1, p. 8.

21. Pétrement, *A Life,* p. 205.

22. Ibid., p. 213.

5: The Year of Factory Work, 1934–35

1. Staughton Lynd, "The First New Left, and the Third," in *Simone Weil: Interpretations of a Life,* edited by George Abbott White (Amherst: University of Massachusetts Press, 1981), pp. 110–11.

2. Simone Weil, *La Condition Ouvrière* (Paris: Gallimard, 1951), pp. 19–20.

3. Ibid., p. 47.

4. Ibid., p. 37.

5. Ibid., p. 65.

6. Ibid., p. 67.

7. Ibid., p. 65.

8. Ibid., p. 21.

9. Ibid., p. 162.

10. Ibid., p. 24.

11. Ibid., p. 21.

12. Ibid., p. 148.

13. Ibid., p. 15.

14. Ibid., p. 80.

15. Ibid., p. 85.

16. Ibid., p. 82.

17. Ibid., p. 81 (emphasis Weil's).

18. Ibid., p. 82.

19. Ibid., p. 20.

20. Ibid., p. 22.

21. Ibid., p. 50.

22. Ibid., p. 83.

23. Ibid., p. 148.

24. Ibid., pp. 106–7.

25. Ibid., pp. 166–67.

26. Ibid., p. 86.

27. Pétrement, *A Life,* p. 240.

28. Weil, *La Condition Ouvrière,* pp. 89–90.

29. Ibid., p. 99.

30. Ibid., p. 92.

31. Ibid., p. 96.

32. Ibid., p. 104.

33. Ibid., p. 98.

34. Ibid., p. 24.

35. Ibid., p. 55.

36. Ibid., p. 21.

37. Weil, *Waiting for God,* p. 66.

38. Weil, *La Condition Ouvrière,* p. 16.

39. Quoted in George Abbott White, editor, *Simone Weil: Interpretations of a Life* (Amherst: University of Massachusetts Press, 1981), p. 171.

40. Weil, *La Condition Ouvrière,* p. 242.

41. Ibid., pp. 215–16.

6: The Budding of Faith, 1935–38

1. Weil, *Waiting for God,* p. 67.

2. Pétrement, *A Life,* p. 250.

3. Ibid., p. 259.

4. Ibid., p. 203.

5. Ibid., p. 261.

6. Ibid., p. 264.

7. Weil, *La Condition Ouvrière*, pp. 169–70.

8. McLellan, *Utopian Pessimist*, p. 120.

9. Pétrement, *A Life*, p. 274.

10. Simone Weil, *Oeuvres*, quarto edition (Paris: Gallimard, 1999), "Lettre à Georges Bernanos," p. 409.

11. Pétrement, French edition, pp. 408–9.

12. Plato's reference to the "Great Beast" (*"gros animal"* in Weil's translation from the Greek) occurs in book 6 of *The Republic*, II. 492–94.

13. All these citations come from letters 1–3 from Simone Weil to Jean Posternak, written in 1937 and published in *Cahiers Simone Weil*, vol. X, no. 2 (June 1987).

14. *Waiting for God*, pp. 67–68.

15. McLellan, *Utopian Pessimist*, p. 133.

16. Pétrement, French edition, pp. 467–68.

17. Letter 5 to Jean Posternak, late March/early April 1938, published in *Cahiers Simone Weil*, vol. X, no. 2 (June 1987).

7: Toward God and War, 1938–39

1. Pétrement, *A Life*, p. 329.

2. Weil, *Waiting for God*, p. 68.

3. McLellan, *Utopian Pessimist*, p. 137.

4. Simone Weil, *Seventy Letters*, translated by Richard Rees (Oxford: Oxford University Press, 1965), p. 140.

5. Ibid.

6. Weil, *Waiting for God*, p. 69.

7. Blaise Pascal, *Pensées*, edited by Léon Brunschvicg (Paris: Garnier-Flammarion, 1976), pp. 43–44. (Pascal's "Memorial," barely one page long, is the opening selection in most contemporary editions of the *Pensées*.)

8. Pétrement, *A Life*, p. 329.

9. Ibid., p. 326.

10. Simone Weil, *Formative Writings, 1929–1941*, edited and translated by Dorothy Tuck McFarland and Wilhelmina Van Ness (London: Routledge & Kegan Paul, 1987), p. 265.

11. Pétrement, *A Life*, p. 327.

12. Ibid., p. 337.

8: The Debacle

1. André Weil, *The Apprenticeship of a Mathematician*, p. 126.

2. Weil, *Oeuvres*, quarto edition, pp. 367–85.

3. Simone Weil, *Notebooks*, vol. 2, translated by Arthur Wills (London: Routledge & Kegan Paul, 1956), p. 568.

4. Weil, *Seventy Letters*, p. 129.

5. Weil, *Waiting for God*, p. 145.

6. Jacques Cabaud, *Simone Weil à New York et à Londres: Les Quinze Derniers Mois (1942–1943)* (Paris: Librairie Plon, 1967), p. 29.

7. André Maurois, "Tragédie en France" (New York: Éditions de la Maison Française, n.d.), p. 98

8. Pétrement, French edition, p. 381.

9. Weil, *Oeuvres*, quarto edition, pp. 671–80.

9: Marseilles

1. Pétrement, *A Life*, pp. 391–92.

2. Anna Freud, quoted in Robert Coles, *Simone Weil: A Modern Pilgrimage* (Reading, Mass.: Addison-Wesley, 1987), p. 58.

3. Jean Améry, *At the Mind's Limits: Contemplations by a Survivor of Auschwitz and Its Realities* (Bloomington: Indiana University Press, 1980), p. 94.

4. Pétrement, French edition, p. 530.

5. Pétrement, *A Life*, p. 407.

6. *Cahiers Simone Weil*, March–April 1986, pp. 1, 11.

7. Pétrement, *A Life*, p. 422.

8. *Cahiers Simone Weil*, vol. II, no. 4 (December 1979), p. 179, cited in McLellan, *Utopian Pessimist*, p. 173.

9. Joseph-Marie Perrin and Gustave Thibon, *Simone Weil as We Knew Her* (London: Routledge & Kegan Paul, 1953), p. 124.

10. Simone Weil, *Gravity and Grace*, translated by Emma Craufurd (New York and London: Routledge Press, 1963), pp. vii–xxxvii.

11. Pétrement, *A Life*, p. 426.

12. Perrin and Thibon, *Simone Weil as We Knew Her*, p. 116.

13. *Twentieth-Century Literary Criticism*, vol. 23 (Detroit: Gale Publishing Co., 1987), p. 382.

14. Pétrement, *A Life*, p. 435.

15. Weil, *Waiting for God*, pp. 71–72.

16. Pétrement, French edition, p. 589.

17. Pétrement, *A Life*, p. 442.

18. Weil, *Oeuvres*, quarto edition, pp. 973–74.

19. Pétrement, *A Life*, p. 447.

20. Weil, *Waiting for God*, pp. 43–51.

21. Ibid., p. 55.

22. *Cahiers Simone Weil,* March–April 1986.

23. Pétrement, *A Life,* p. 457.

24. Ibid., p. 470.

25. Ibid., p. 474.

10: New York

1. Pétrement, *A Life,* p. 396.

2. Ibid., p. 476.

3. Ibid., p. 475.

4. Ibid., p. 480.

5. Cabaud, *Simone Weil à New York et à Londres,* p. 35.

6. Simone Weil, *First and Last Notebooks,* translated by Richard Rees (New York and Toronto: Oxford University Press, 1970), p. 144.

7. Ibid., pp. 243–44.

8. Pétrement, *A Life,* p. 478.

9. Weil, *Seventy Letters,* p. 157.

10. Pétrement, French edition, p. 641.

11. Weil, *Oeuvres,* quarto edition, pp. 985–1015.

12. Pétrement, *A Life,* p. 489.

11: London

1. Pétrement, *A Life,* p. 511.

2. Simone Weil, *The Need for Roots: Prelude to a Declaration of Duties Toward Mankind,* translated by Arthur Wills (New York: G. P. Putnam's Sons, 1952), pp. 4–5.

3. Ibid., p. 26.

4. Weil, *Waiting for God,* p. 97.

5. See Conor Cruise O'Brien, Weil entry in *Twentieth-Century Literary Criticism,* vol. 23, pp. 398–401.

6. Pétrement, *A Life,* p. 510.

7. Ibid., p. 509.

8. Ibid., p. 518

9. Weil, *Seventy Letters,* p. 177.

10. Cabaud, *A Fellowship in Love,* p. 340; McLellan, *Utopian Pessimist,* pp. 262–63; Pétrement, *A Life,* p. 523.

11. Pétrement, *A Life,* p. 531.

12. Ibid., p. 535.

13. Weil, *First and Last Notebooks,* pp. 361–62.

14. Ibid., p. 364.

15. Ibid., p. 286.

16. Pétrement, *A Life,* p. 537.

17. Author's conversation with Simone Weil's niece, Sylvie Weil, New York City, April 2000.

12: Our Father Who Art in Secret

1. Weil, *Gravity and Grace,* p. 33.

2. Ibid., p. 24.

3. Ibid., p. 27.

4. Ibid., p. 82.

5. Ibid., p. 47.

6. Weil, *Waiting for God,* p. 83.

7. Weil, *Gravity and Grace,* p. 10.

Notes

8. Ibid., p. 132.

9. Ibid., p. 49.

10. Ibid., p. 15.

11. Ibid., p. 19.

12. Weil, *Waiting for God,* p. 212.

13. Ibid., p. 138.

14. Ibid., p. 144.

15. Ibid., p. 143.

16. Ibid., p. 184.

17. Ibid., p. 165.

18. Ibid., pp. 168–69.

19. Ibid., p. 121.

20. Ibid., p. 132.

21. Weil, *Gravity and Grace,* p. 106.

22. Weil, *Waiting for God,* p. 196.

23. Ibid., pp. 194–95.

24. Weil, *Gravity and Grace,* p. 136.

25. Weil, *Waiting for God,* p. 166.

26. Ibid., pp. 163–64.

27. Ibid., p. 93.

28. Ibid., p. 210. (I've taken particularly extensive liberties in correcting syntactical infelicities in this passage of the Harper Perennial Library edition.)

29. Ibid., pp. 199–200.

30. T. S. Eliot, preface to Weil, *The Need for Roots* (New York: G. P. Putnam's Sons, 1952), pp. v–xii.

31. Gabriel Marcel, "Simone Weil," *The Month* 2, no. 1 (July 1949), p. 18.

32. Graham Greene, *Collected Essays* (New York: Viking Press, 1969), p. 375.

33. Leslie Fiedler, introduction to Weil, *Waiting for God* (New York: G. P. Putnam's Sons, 1951), p. 3.

34. Alfred Kazin, *The Inmost Leaf: A Selection of Essays* (New York: Harcourt Brace Jovanovich, 1955), pp. 208–13.

35. See Kenneth Rexroth, Weil entry in *Twentieth-Century Literary Criticism,* vol. 23, p. 382.

36. Hans Meyerhoff, "Contra Simone Weil: The Voice of Demons for the Silence of God," in *Arguments and Doctrines: A Reader of Jewish Thinking in the Aftermath of the Holocaust,* edited by Arthur A. Cohen (New York: Harper & Row, 1970), pp. 70–85.

37. Czeslaw Milosz, *Emperor of the Earth: Modes of Eccentric Vision* (Berkeley: University of California Press, 1977), pp. 85–98.

38. Conor Cruise O'Brien, "The Anti-Politics of Simone Weil," *New York Review of Books,* May 12, 1977, pp. 23–28.

39. Susan Sontag, *Against Interpretation* (New York: Farrar, Straus & Giroux and Dell Publishing Co., 1961), pp. 58–59.

40. Weil, *Cahiers,* vol. 3 (Paris: Plon, 1970–74), pp. 291–92.

Bibliography

Works by Simone Weil

Attente de Dieu. Paris: Editions du Vieux-Colombier, 1950.

Cahiers, 3 vols. Paris: Plon, 1970–74.

La Condition Ouvrière. Collection Espoir, dirigée par Albert Camus. Paris: Gallimard, 1951.

First and Last Notebooks. Translated by Richard Rees. New York/ Toronto: Oxford University Press, 1970.

Formative Writings, 1929–1941. Edited and translated by Dorothy Tuck McFarland and Wilhelmina Van Ness. London: Routledge & Kegan Paul, 1987.

Gravity and Grace. Translated by Emma Craufurd. New York/London: Routledge Press, 1963.

Intimations of Christianity Among the Ancient Greeks. Translator unnamed. New York/London: Routledge Press, 1998.

Lectures on Philosophy. Translated by Hugh Price and introduced by Peter Winch. Cambridge, England: Cambridge University Press, 1978.

The Need for Roots: Prelude to a Declaration of Duties Toward Mankind. Translated by Arthur Wills. New York: G. P. Putnam's Sons, 1952.

Notebooks. Translated from the French by Arthur Wills. 2 vols. London: Routledge & Kegan Paul, 1956.

Oeuvres. Quarto edition. Sous la direction de Florence de Lussy. Paris: Gallimard, 1999.

Oeuvres Complètes. Sous la direction d'André A. Devaux et de Florence de Lussy. Paris: Gallimard, 1991–2000.

Oppression and Liberty. Translated by Arthur Wills. London: Routledge & Kegan Paul, 1958.

Bibliography

Oppression et Liberté. Paris: Gallimard, 1955.

La Pesanteur et la Grace. Paris: Plon, 1948.

Selected Essays, 1934–1943. Translated by Richard Rees. Oxford: Oxford University Press, 1962.

Seventy Letters. Translated by Richard Rees. Oxford: Oxford University Press, 1965.

Simone Weil: An Anthology. Edited by Siân Miles. New York: Weidenfeld & Nicolson, 1986.

The Simone Weil Reader. Edited by George A. Panichas. Wakefield, R.I./London: Moyer Bell Limited, 1977.

Waiting for God. Translated by Emma Craufurd. New York: G. P. Putnam's Sons, 1951.

Books on Simone Weil

Allen, Diogenes. *Three Outsiders: Pascal, Kierkegaard, Simone Weil.* New York: Cowley Publications, 1983.

Brenner, Rachel Feldhay. *Writing as Resistance: Four Women Confronting the Holocaust: Edith Stein, Simone Weil, Anne Frank, Etty Hillesum.* Unversity Park: Pennsylvania State University Press, 1997.

Breuck, Katherine T. *The Redemption of Tragedy: The Literary Vision of Simone Weil.* Albany: State University of New York Press, 1995.

Cabaud, Jacques. *Simone Weil: A Fellowship in Love.* Des Moines/New York: Channel Press, 1964.

———. *Simone Weil à New York et à Londres: Les Quinze Derniers Mois (1942–1943).* Paris: Librairie Plon, 1967.

Cohen, Arthur A., ed. *Arguments and Doctrines: A Reader of Jewish Thinking in the Aftermath of the Holocaust.* New York: Harper & Row, 1970.

Coles, Robert. *Simone Weil: A Modern Pilgrimage.* Reading, Mass.: Addison-Wesley, 1987.

Dargan, Joan. *Simone Weil: Thinking Poetically.* Albany: State University of New York Press, 1999.

Debidour, V. H. *Simone Weil, ou la transparence.* Paris: Librairie Plon, 1963.

Dunaway, John M. *Simone Weil.* Boston: Twayne Publishers, 1984.

Dunaway, John M., and Eric O. Springsted, eds. *The Beauty That Saves: Essays on Aesthetics and Language in Simone Weil.* Macon, Ga.: Mercer University Press, 1996.

Bibliography

Finch, Henry Leroy. *Simone Weil and the Intellect of Grace.* New York: Continuum Publishing Company, 1999.

Fiori, Gabriella. *Simone Weil: Biografia di un pensiero.* Milan: Garzanti Editore, 1981.

———. *Simone Weil: An Intellectual Biography.* Translated by Joseph R. Berrigan, Athens/London: University of Georgia Press, 1989.

———. *Simone Weil: Une Femme Absolue.* Paris: Éditions du Félin, 1993.

Greene, Graham. *Collected Essays.* New York: Viking Press, 1969.

Hourdin, Georges. *Simone Weil.* Paris: Éditions La Decourverte, 1989.

Jacquier, Charles, ed. *Simone Weil, l'expérience de la vie et le travail de la pensée.* Arles: Éditions Sulliver, 1998.

Kazin, Alfred. *The Inmost Leaf: A Selection of Essays.* New York: Harcourt Brace Jovanovich, 1955.

McLellan, David. *Simone Weil: Utopian Pessimist.* London: Macmillan Press, 1989.

Milosz, Czeslaw. *Emperor of the Earth: Modes of Eccentric Vision.* Berkeley: University of California Press, 1977.

Nevin, Thomas R. *Simone Weil: Portrait of a Self-Hating Jew.* Chapel Hill: University of North Carolina Press, 1991.

Oxenhandler, Neal. *Looking for Heroes in Postwar France: Albert Camus, Max Jacob, Simone Weil.* Hanover, N.H./London: University Press of New England, 1996.

Perrin, Joseph-Marie, and Gustave Thibon. *Simone Weil as We Knew Her.* London: Routledge & Kegan Paul, 1953.

Pétrement, Simone. *La Vie de Simone Weil.* Paris: Librairie Arthème Fayard, 1973.

———. *Simone Weil: A Life.* Translated by Raymond Rosenthal. New York: Pantheon Books, 1976.

Piccard, E. *Simone Weil: Essai Biographique et Critique.* Paris: Presses Universitaires de France, 1960.

Plant, Stephen. *Simone Weil.* Liguori, Miss.: Triumph Books, 1996.

Saint-Robert, Phillipe de. *La Vision Tragique de Simone Weil.* Paris François-Xavier de Guibert, 1999.

Sontag, Susan. *Against Interpretation.* New York: Farrar, Straus & Giroux and Dell Publishing Co., 1961.

Tomlin, E. W. F. *Simone Weil.* New Haven, Conn.: Yale University Press 1954.

Bibliography

Twentieth-Century Literary Criticism. Vol. 23, pp. 363–405. Detroit: Gale Research Company, 1987.

White, George Abbott, ed. *Simone Weil: Interpretations of a Life.* Amherst: University of Massachusetts Press, 1981.

Winch, Peter. *Simone Weil: The Just Balance.* Cambridge and New York: Cambridge University Press, 1989.

General Background

Alder, Alexandre, and Bernard Cohen. *Juif et Juif.* Paris: Éditions Autrement, 1985.

Améry, Jean. *At the Mind's Limits: Contemplations by a Survivor of Auschwitz and Its Realities.* Bloomington: Indiana University Press, 1980.

Aron, Raymond. *The Opium of the Intellectuals.* Garden City, N.Y.: Doubleday, 1957.

de Beauvoir, Simone. *Memoirs of a Dutiful Daughter.* New York: Harper & Row, 1974.

Bell, Rudolph M. *Holy Anorexia.* Chicago/London: University of Chicago Press, 1985.

Bloch, Marc. *The Strange Defeat.* New York: W.W. Norton, 1999.

Counihan, Carole M. *The Anthropology of Food and Body: Gender, Meaning, and Power.* New York/London: Routledge, 1999.

Finkielkraut, Alain. *Le Mécontemporain: Péguy, lecteur du monde moderne.* Paris: Éditions Gallimard, 1991.

Glück, Louise. *Proofs and Theories.* New York: Ecco Press, 1994.

Hughes, H. Stuart. *The Obstructed Path: French Social Thought in the Years of Desperation, 1930–1960.* Evanston, Ill./New York: Harper & Row, 1968.

Judt, Tony. *The Burden of Responsibility: Blum, Camus, Aron, and the French Twentieth Century.* Chicago/London: University of Chicago Press, 1997.

Kaplan, Louise J. *Adolescence: The Farewell to Childhood.* New York: Simon & Schuster, 1987.

Kelly, Michael. *Modern French Marxism.* Baltimore: Johns Hopkins University Press, 1982.

Maître, Jacques. *Anorexies Religieuses et Anorexie Mentale: Essai de psychanalyse sociohistorique de Marie de l'Incarnation à Simone Weil.* Paris: Éditions du Cerf, 2000.

Bibliography

Maurois, André. *Tragédie en France*. New York: Éditions de la Maison Française, n.d.

Micaud, Charles A. *Communism and the French Left*. New York: Frederick A. Praeger, 1963.

Noguères, Henri. *La Vie quotidienne au temps du Front populaire, 1935–1938*. Paris: Hachette, 1977.

Ory, Pascal, and Jean-François Sirinelli. *Les Intellectuels en France, de l'Affair Dreyfus à nos jours*. Paris: Armand Colin, 1986.

Pascal, Blaise. *Pensées*. Edited by Léon Brunschvicg. Paris: Garnier-Flammarion, 1976.

Peignot, Jérôme, and Anne Roche, eds. *Laure: Une Rupture*. Paris: Éditions des Cendres, 1999.

Roche, Anne. *Boris Souvarine et La Critique Sociale*. Paris: Éditions La Découverte, 1990.

Touchard, Jean. *La gauche en France depuis 1990*. Paris: Éditions du Seuil, 1977.

Weil, André. *André Weil: The Apprenticeship of a Mathematician*. Translated by Jennifer Gage. Basel/Boston/Berlin: Birkhäuser Verlag, 1992.

Periodicals

Cahiers Simone Weil. Published by the Association for the Study of Simone Weil's Thought, Passy, France, 1978–.

Horgan, John. "The Last Universal Mathematician." *Scientific American*, June 1994, pp. 33–34.

Julliard, Jacques. "La Trollesse de Dieu." *Nouvel Observateur*, May 13–19, 1999.

Marcel, Gabriel. "Simone Weil." *The Month* 2, no. 1 (July 1949), p. 18

O'Brien, Conor Cruise. "The Anti-Politics of Simone Weil." *New York Review of Books*, May 12, 1977.

Pirruccello, Ann. "Interpreting Simone Weil: Presence and Absence in Attention." *Philosophy East and West* 45, no. 1 (January 1995), pp. 61–74.

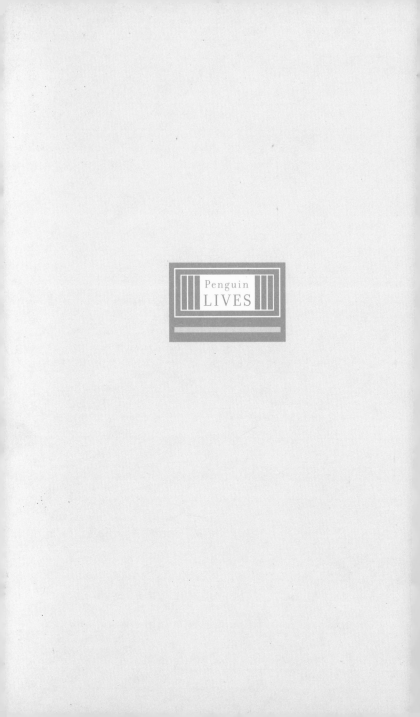

Penguin
LIVES